THE BUFFALO
HUNTERS

✤

TIME® LIFE BOOKS

This volume is one of a series that chronicles the history and culture of the Native Americans. Other books in the series include:

THE FIRST AMERICANS
THE SPIRIT WORLD
THE EUROPEAN CHALLENGE
PEOPLE OF THE DESERT
THE WAY OF THE WARRIOR

The Cover: A leader of the Mandan Buffalo Bull Society, a prestigious warrior league, wears a buffalo head mask and carries a shield and ceremonial lance in preparation for the Buffalo Bull Dance in this 1834 watercolor by Karl Bodmer. Almost all of the Plains tribes relied on the buffalo for food, clothing, and shelter, and held annual ceremonies to honor the animal that was so essential to their well-being.

THE BUFFALO HUNTERS

✤

by
THE EDITORS
of
TIME-LIFE BOOKS

ALEXANDRIA, VIRGINIA

TIME-LIFE BOOKS

EDITOR-IN-CHIEF: Thomas H. Flaherty
Director of Editorial Resources: Elise D. Ritter-Clough
Executive Art Director: Ellen Robling
Director of Photography and Research:
John Conrad Weiser
Editorial Board: Dale M. Brown, Janet Cave,
Roberta Conlan, Robert Doyle, Laura Foreman,
Jim Hicks, Rita Thievon Mullin, Henry Woodhead
Assistant Director of Editorial Resources:
Norma E. Shaw

PRESIDENT: John D. Hall

Vice President and Director of Marketing:
Nancy K. Jones
Editorial Director: Russell B. Adams, Jr.
Director of Production Services: Robert N. Carr
Production Manager: Marlene Zack
Director of Technology: Eileen Bradley
Supervisor of Quality Control: James King

Editorial Operations
Production: Celia Beattie
Library: Louise D. Forstall
Computer Composition: Deborah G. Tait (Manager),
Monika D. Thayer, Janet Barnes Syring,
Lillian Daniels
Interactive Media Specialist: Patti H. Cass

Time-Life Books is a division of Time Life Incorporated

PRESIDENT AND CEO: John M. Fahey, Jr.

Library of Congress Cataloging in Publication Data
The Buffalo hunters/by the editors of Time-
Life Books.
    p. cm. — (The American Indians)
    Includes bibliographical references and index.
    ISBN 0-8094-9425-6
    ISBN 0-8094-9426-4 (lib. bdg.)
    1. Indians of North America—Great Plains—
Social life and customs. 2. Indians of North
America—Great Plains—Domestic animals.
3. Horses—Social aspects—Great Plains.
4. Bison, American—Social aspects—Great Plains.
I. Time-Life Books. II. Series.
E78.G73B78 1993   92-39726
978'.00497—dc20   CIP

THE AMERICAN INDIANS

SERIES EDITOR: Henry Woodhead
Administrative Editor: Jane Edwin

Editorial Staff for *The Buffalo Hunters:*
Senior Art Directors: Herbert H. Quarmby (principal),
Dale Pollekoff, Ray Ripper
Picture Editor: Susan V. Kelly
Text Editors: John Newton (principal),
Stephen G. Hyslop
Writers: Maggie Debelius, Stephanie Lewis
Associate Editors/Research: Harris J. Andrews
(principal), Mary Helena McCarthy, Quentin Gaines
Story, Marilyn Murphy Terrell
Assistant Editor/Research: Annette Scarpitta
Assistant Art Director: Susan M. Gibas
Senior Copyeditor: Ann Lee Bruen
Picture Coordinator: David Beard
Editorial Assistant: Gemma Villanueva

Special Contributors: Ronald H. Bailey, Charles S.
Clark, George G. Daniels, Marfé Ferguson Delano,
Susan Perry, Peter Pocock, Lydia Preston, David S.
Thomson (text); Martha Lee Beckington, Barbara
Fleming, Elizabeth Pope, Jennifer Veech (research);
Barbara L. Klein (index).

Correspondents: Elisabeth Kraemer-Singh (Bonn),
Christine Hinze (London), Christina Lieberman
(New York), Maria Vincenza Aloisi (Paris), Ann
Natanson (Rome). Valuable assistance was also
provided by: Elizabeth Brown, Katheryn White
(New York).

General Consultants
Frederick E. Hoxie is director of the D'Arcy McNickle
Center for the History of the American Indian at the
Newberry Library in Chicago. Dr. Hoxie is the author
of *A Final Promise: The Campaign to Assimilate the
Indians 1880-1920* and other works. He has served
as a history consultant to the Cheyenne River and
Standing Rock Sioux tribes, Little Big Horn College
archives, and the Senate Select Committee on Indian
Affairs. He is a trustee of the National Museum of the
American Indian in Washington, D.C.

Darrell Robes Kipp, a Blackfeet and great-grandson of
Chief Heavy Runner, is a founder and director of the
Piegan Institute in Browning, Montana, a private,
nonprofit, tribally chartered organization that
researches, promotes, and preserves Native American
languages, specifically the Blackfeet language. A
graduate of Eastern Montana College and Harvard
University, Mr. Kipp has for many years served his
tribe as a teacher, administrator, technical writer, and
historian. He has also worked for the Maliseet Indian
tribe of New Brunswick, Canada, the Navajo, and the
Confederated Assiniboin and Gros Ventre tribes,
among others. Mr. Kipp has written articles and produced materials for video on the Blackfeet tribe.

Special Consultants
Michael Crummett is a freelance photographer and
writer from Billings, Montana, whose work has appeared in numerous books and periodicals, including
the Smithsonian *Handbook of the North American
Indian* series and *American Heritage* and *Traveler*
magazines. He began working with the Crow Indians
as a Vista volunteer in 1971 and has expanded this
interest to other Montana tribes. He provided the
photographs for *Montana's Indians: Yesterday and
Today* and is the author of *Big Day Golden Year: The
Fiftieth Anniversary of the Crow Indian Sun Dance.*

Brenda Margaret Farnell, Visiting Assistant Professor
of Anthropology at the University of Iowa, has
focused her research on linguistic and symbolic anthropology and semiotics. Dr. Farnell has presented
numerous papers and lectured frequently on these
topics, especially as they pertain to Native American
cultures. She is the author of *"Do You See What I
Mean?": Plains Indian Sign Talk and the Embodiment
of Action.*

Patricia A. McCormack is Curator of Ethnology at the
Provincial Museum of Alberta and an adjunct professor in the Department of Anthropology at the University of Alberta in Edmonton, Canada. She has done
extensive research among the Blackfeet relating to
their religion and horse traditions and has also stud-
ied the history and culture of the Chipewyan, Cree,
and Metis peoples. She has written extensively on
these subjects for scholarly journals and general publications.

Dale Old Horn is Department Head of Crow Studies
and Social Sciences at Little Big Horn College in
Crow Agency, Montana, and a graduate of the Massachusetts Institute of Technology. A Crow Indian,
Professor Old Horn has been a visiting lecturer at
many colleges and universities, including Michigan
State University and the University of Wisconsin, and
has served as master of ceremonies for numerous
powwows, among them the Crow Fair and the United Tribes International. He is also a contributor to
scholarly journals.

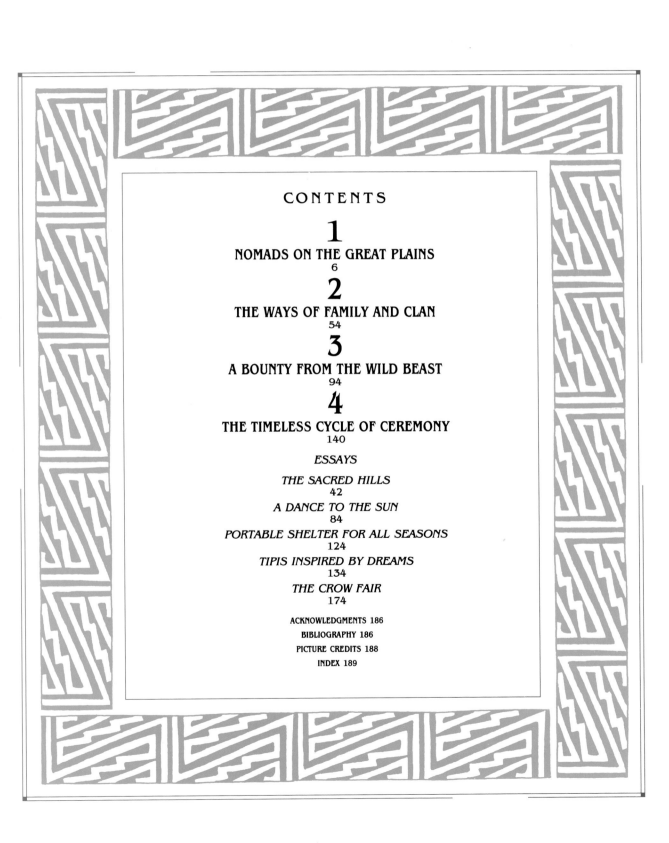

CONTENTS

1
NOMADS ON THE GREAT PLAINS
6

2
THE WAYS OF FAMILY AND CLAN
54

3
A BOUNTY FROM THE WILD BEAST
94

4
THE TIMELESS CYCLE OF CEREMONY
140

ESSAYS

1

NOMADS ON THE GREAT PLAINS

In 1913, when the American sculptor James Earle Fraser designed a new five-cent piece for the United States Mint, he decided to pay homage to a people whose remarkable way of life had already disappeared. Fraser had grown up among the Indians of the Dakota prairies, and he took as his models three chiefs who had lived the glory days on the Great Plains. From their countenances he created on the head of the new nickel a composite profile of an Indian with high cheekbones, aquiline nose, and braided hair adorned with eagle feathers.

Here was the classic Indian. Fraser's striking portrait conjured up romantic visions of free-spirited warriors galloping across an open range under the immense western sky. In fact, to millions of Americans, the craggy profile grew so familiar that it came to symbolize all Indians.

But Fraser knew that the Plains Indians were a breed apart, and he knew what had made them unique. On the opposite side of his Indian-head nickel, he put a portrait of the shaggy-maned, humpbacked creature that had stood at the center of life on the Plains for thousands of years. Scientists know the species as *Bison bison*. To almost everyone else, it is the American buffalo. Not really a buffalo at all, the meaty animal had acquired that name because French explorers had called it *boeuf,* for beef, and unschooled English-speaking frontiersmen had taken it from there.

The juxtaposition of these two images could not have been more fitting. The fate of the Plains Indian and the buffalo were inextricably intertwined. Rarely has the dependence on a single animal so dominated and shaped human lives. From this magnificent creature, standing up to six feet tall at the shoulder and weighing as much as one ton, the Indians obtained practically every necessity of life. In addition to providing huge quantities of meat and the dung for fuel to cook it, the buffalo yielded hides for raiment and shelter—and brain paste for tanning them—tallow to burn for light, horns for spoons and other utensils, bones for tools, bladders for containers, hair for ropes, and tendons for bowstrings. The Indians even found use for the hoofs, turning them into ceremonial rat-

Verdant expanses such as this wind-swept sea of grass in Kansas once sustained plentiful herds of buffalo that furnished the native peoples of the Great Plains with almost every essential of life. The grateful Indians honored the animal in solemn ceremonies, including the Sun Dance, an annual ritual of sacrifice and thanksgiving conducted around a pole crowned with a buffalo skull.

OMAHA ELDER

ASSINIBOIN MAN

More than two dozen distinct tribes found homes on the sweeping grasslands between the Mississippi River and the Rocky Mountains, bringing with them a multiplicity of languages, customs, and adornments. As portrayed here in early-20th-century photographs, these diverse peoples—from the village-dwelling Omaha and Hidatsa to the nomadic Kiowa and Cheyenne—made the Plains America's original melting pot.

tles to beseech the sacred powers to ensure successful buffalo hunting.

The people who built a distinctive way of life around the buffalo were many and diverse. They belonged to 32 tribes from a half-dozen language groups. So dissimilar were the tongues in which they spoke that they could communicate across tribal boundaries only with sign language. They were the inheritors of two highly evolved cultural traditions. Some were agriculturists who had migrated from the eastern woodlands to settle the bottom lands along the great rivers and their tributaries. Others were migratory hunter-gatherers. Both groups proved extraordinarily adaptable—the farmers becoming part-time hunters, and a few of the nomadic hunters picking up the rudiments of agriculture. All of the Plains dwellers possessed resilient cultures, absorbing new tools and technologies while clinging tenaciously to the core of their ancient traditions.

By 1780, at the dawn of their era of maximum expansion, perhaps 400,000 persons inhabited the Plains, scattered over a region of nearly one million square miles, reaching from the foothills of the Rocky Mountains eastward to the woodlands of the Mississippi Valley, and from what is today central Texas northward to Alberta, Saskatchewan, and Manitoba. For at least part of the year, the movement of the nomadic tribes mirrored the migrations of the buffalo. The hunters lived in the conic tents known as tipis, hunted on horseback, and shared many sacred ceremonies. The farming groups, who erected permanent dwellings along the rivers of present-day western Minnesota, Iowa, and Missouri, limited

STRIKES TWO, ARIKARA

HIDATSA MOTHER AND CHILD

travel to extended hunting expeditions to supplement their largely vegetarian diet with the valuable protein offered by the buffalo.

To a large extent, natural forces dictated the routine of life on the Plains. It was the abundant rainfall of up to 40 inches annually that allowed the easternmost tribes to grow corn. Farther westward, rainfall decreased to 10 inches or less annually, and the grass grew shorter. But it was hardy pasturage, growing quickly on spring moisture and then curing naturally into nutritious forage for the buffalo.

Seasonal variations in the weather were unpredictable and fraught with danger for the Plains inhabitants. Summer brought violent thunderstorms and tornadoes; winter, fierce blizzards with immense snowfall. In a single day, temperatures could fluctuate as many as 50 degrees. After months of drought, the sky might suddenly blacken and disgorge torrents of blinding rain, or icy sheets of hail. At other times, searing gale-strength winds raged out of the south, like the blast of a hot furnace, to wither the grass and threaten every growing thing.

But more than anything, the presence of the buffalo was the key to human occupancy of the Plains. The gigantic herds roaming the vast range matched the immensity of land and sky, darkening the horizon for miles on end and defying enumeration. In the words of the 19th-century American zoologist William T. Hornaday: "It would have been as easy to count or to estimate the number of leaves in a forest as to calculate the number of buffaloes living at any given time previous to 1870."

GRIZZLY BEAR, PIEGAN

BLACKFEET WOMAN

The Plains were alive with movement: migrating animals, windblown mountains of clouds, rippling oceans of grass. The people, too, had been rovers. Driven by weather, fluctuations in climate, and the need to hunt, they crisscrossed the prairies, leaving behind trails of animal bones, spearpoints, and other traces of their campsites. Sometimes drought or warfare forced them to move off the Plains. But newcomers kept arriving, who were in turn shaped in the crucible of their new way of life.

Although the origin histories of all Plains tribes place their roots in North America, most scholars contend that the earliest inhabitants of the Plains were descendants of the first Americans who crossed from the Old World to the New World during the Ice Age, perhaps 15,000 years ago, on a land bridge that briefly connected Siberia with Alaska. This temporary link was forged when the great glaciers blanketing the northern reaches of North America absorbed sufficient water to lower the level of the Bering Strait, exposing the sea bottom. As the glaciers receded, opening a corridor south, the migrants made their way from Alaska and northern Canada onto the Great Plains. There, they found a hunter's paradise inhabited by such Ice Age behemoths as the camel, giant bison, woolly mammoth, and a native species of the horse.

Although these mammals gradually grew extinct—probably because of changes in climate or overhunting—the Plains supplied a new quarry for the nomadic bands of Indians. The modern bison, a smaller version of earlier species that had disappeared, emerged about 7,000 years ago. Per-

BOY IN THE WATER, CROW

TWO BEARS, SIOUX

haps moving north to escape the climatic changes that reduced the Mexican grasslands to desert scrub, the buffalo found an ideal home on the lush greensward. The Indians, in turn, found a source of subsistence that would sustain them and their progeny for seven millennia.

To bring down the buffalo and their bigger predecessors, Plains hunters put together an arsenal of weapons and techniques that endured until the introduction of the horse and gun after the 17th century. The Indians augmented their stone-tipped thrusting spear with the atlatl, or spearthrower; a shaft of wood or bone about two feet long, the device cradled a short spear or dart and enabled the hunter to fling it farther and with greater striking power than would have been possible using his arm alone. Hunters learned to ambush their quarry at water holes and to stalk the herds in disguise. Several hunters would don bison robes or even the skin of a wolf—a predator whose presence was familiar to the buffalo—and creep close enough to drive home their spears.

In addition to these techniques, the early hunters developed methods of mass killing. By shouting and brandishing their weapons, or by setting the grass ablaze, they stampeded entire herds into box canyons and dry ravines where the buffalo became easy targets. In one such instance of wholesale slaughter that occurred in eastern Colorado 8,500 years ago, no fewer than 193 bison died, yielding an estimated 30 tons of meat.

Indian pioneers on the western Plains also developed a hunting technique called the jump kill. The killing site typically consisted of a high cliff

CHIEF RED WHIP, GROS VENTRE

NI-DA-WI, OMAHA

over which a herd could be stampeded to death. Beginning about 5,600 years ago, and perhaps earlier, a sandstone outcropping some 80 miles south of the present-day Canadian city of Calgary served such a purpose. Hunters funneled their prey to the cliff along converging creek basins up to five miles long and marked by piles of rock. Any creatures that survived the 60-foot plunge were finished off by the hunters waiting below. Their weapons included atlatl-thrown darts and—after the bow and arrow's arrival via fishing tribes living in the vicinity of present-day British Columbia about 500 to 600 BC—delicately flaked chert arrowheads. The cliff was used as recently as 1800 by the Piegan Indians of the Blackfoot Confederacy, who gave the site its vivid name—Head-Smashed-In.

Mass kills were communal enterprises requiring precise teamwork. In all of the Plains, the early population probably never exceeded 10,000 people, and they were dispersed in hundreds of small bands comprising no more than a dozen or so hunters and their families. To procure sufficient meat to survive the winter, several bands would come together for a few weeks, probably in late September, when the buffalo rutting season had just ended and the density of the herds was maximum. Then, after working together for a month or more to achieve a successful slaughter, the group would disperse, resume their pursuit of individual animals, and seek shelter in the valleys and canyons during the worst winter months.

About 4,000 years ago, these bands gained new mobility by domesticating the dog. The Indians draped a crude packsaddle over the dog's

WOLF ROBE, CHEYENNE

KIOWA WARRIOR

shoulders to which they fastened an A-shaped wooden device, consisting of two joined poles that dragged along the ground. French explorers later called the contraption the travois. A sturdy dog could pull a travois loaded with up to 75 pounds of dried meat or other possessions—a capacity that would determine the precise size of the tipi after its development.

The quantity of buffalo fluctuated with prolonged changes in climate. About 7,000 years ago, for example, temperatures gradually rose while rainfall declined. This period of increasing warmth and aridity, which lasted for 2,500 years, destroyed large sections of the southern grasslands and almost certainly forced the herds—and many hunters—to temporarily abandon some areas of the Plains. To make up for the meager numbers of buffalo, people on the edges of the Plains began settling in one place for at least one season of the year. At these campsites, they supplemented their diet by hunting small game and fishing, and by foraging for nuts, berries, tubers, and other wild plants.

The first truly significant departure from the nomadic life, however, came about the first century AD. An influx of migrants from the woodlands east of the Mississippi began to influence the way of life along the rivers on the eastern border of the Plains. In a wide area that included present-day Nebraska, northern Kansas, much of Oklahoma, and territory extending as far west as Colorado, many practices of the eastern woodlands Indians took root. Pottery appeared here for the first time. People as far north as Manitoba began burying their dead in mounds somewhat similar to the larger and more elaborate earthen structures built by the successive cultures in the Ohio Valley that came to be known as Adena and Hopewell, or simply as the mound builders.

During the second or third century AD, people in the tall-grass prairie near today's Kansas City began settling down in small, semipermanent villages for at least part of the year and practicing a rudimentary agriculture. When not hunting deer and small game or out on the grasslands hunting buffalo, they stayed home and cultivated corn and beans at the junction of the Kansas and the Missouri rivers where sediments laid down by the current had built up fertile bottom lands.

Before the beginning of the 10th century, even more substantial settlements sprang up along the Missouri and in other river valleys of the eastern Plains. Hamlets with clusters of earth-covered dwellings contained as many as 100 persons. Rectangular or square in shape, these lodges contained floor space of up to 90 square yards and housed several families. The floor often was two to five feet below the ground; pits for storing crop surpluses were dug even deeper.

Part of the lodge dwellers' diet came from beans, squash, and a new hardier variety of corn that they cultivated in the river-bottom fields. These people continued to depend upon the buffalo, however, and they left home to hunt it for months on end. Their dual existence as both farmer and hunter is best symbolized by the tool they employed to till their gardens—a hoe fashioned from the shoulder blade of the bison.

These villages would eventually be abandoned for reasons that remain murky: Drought may have forced the Indians out, or roving tribes may have raided their corn caches, causing the village dwellers to retreat into the woodlands to the east. In fact, for hundreds of years prior to the 13th century, the Plains region as a whole was sparsely populated. Prolonged drought probably had driven many of the inhabitants into other areas. But augmented by a succession of newcomers, the basic way of life combining hunting and horticulture would endure, coexisting with the full-time nomadic lifestyles that were prevalent farther west.

The 13th century marked the beginning of a population drift that would bring tribes from all directions onto the Plains over the next 600 years. The first group of newcomers who would survive into historic times were the Pawnee. Speakers of a dialect of the Caddoan language family, the Pawnee had long farmed their ancestral lands in what is now east Texas, near the Gulf of Mexico. They and other Caddoan-speaking peoples had

Disguised by wolf skins, two hunters creep within bow-and-arrow range of a buffalo herd in this painting by George Catlin that illustrates one hunting method used before the coming of the horse. Buffalo did not fear wolves and often continued to graze; a skillful hunter could kill several animals before the herd panicked and took flight.

formed a western outpost of the Mississippian mound-building culture that constructed vast ceremonial temples on the flat summits of earthworks. At these temples, priests conducted ritual beheadings and other forms of human sacrifice. When the Pawnee moved north during the 13th century, they took with them the Mississippian farming skills along with hardy new strains of corn that were well suited to cultivation on the Plains. In addition, they brought along their ancient Morning Star ceremony, which included the ritual killing of a captive girl, making them the only Plains culture to practice human sacrifice.

The Pawnee traveled more than 300 miles before settling along the Platte River in southeastern Nebraska. They may have been attracted that far north not only by the rich alluvial soil along the Platte and nearby streams but also by the abundance of buffalo and the sparsity of people.

On the bluffs overlooking the river, the newcomers built large circular lodges with heavy log frames and timber rafters. They covered the frames with layers of dirt and grass, discovering (as would the white pioneers five centuries later) the insulating value of thick prairie sod against winter cold and summer heat. Some of the lodges were big enough to shelter 40

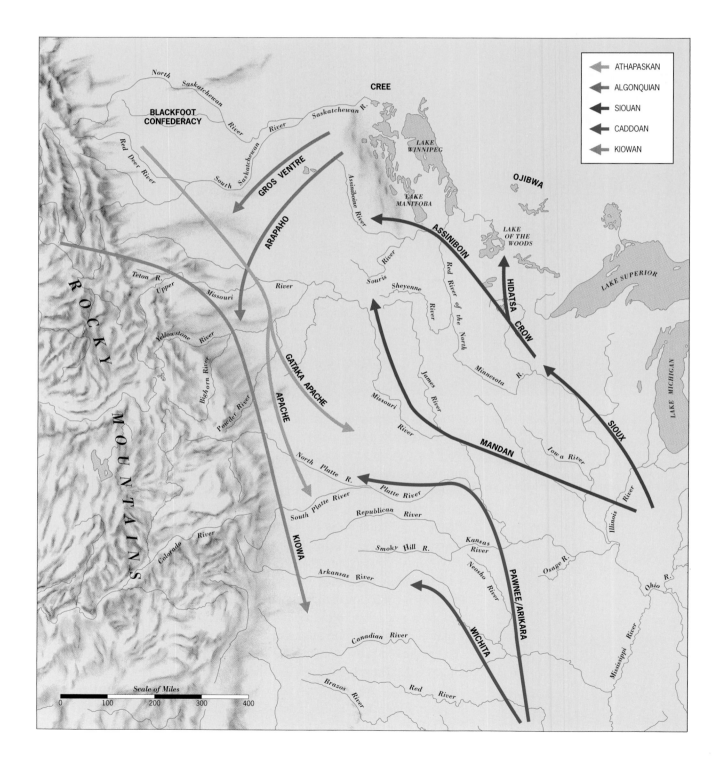

In the 13th century, tribes began to migrate onto the sparsely inhabited Plains from all directions. First to arrive were the Pawnee, a Caddoan-speaking group of farmers who moved into what is now Nebraska from their drought-ridden home in present-day Texas; they were soon followed by the Wichita. By the mid-1400s, the Siouan-speaking Mandan, perhaps responding to population pressures in their Ohio Valley homeland, reached the upper Missouri. As shown on the map at left, several more tribes—including groups from the north speaking Athapaskan and Algonquian languages—flocked to the Plains over the next two centuries.

persons, and the largest villages consisted of up to 15 lodges. By the turn of the 18th century, a few of these villages had expanded to as many as 150 to 300 lodges with total populations of up to 3,000 people. Although these structures were solidly built, the weight of the sod so weakened the timbers that every eight or 10 years they threatened to collapse. By that time, the inhabitants would have depleted the local supply of timber. Thus, every decade or so, the Indians abandoned their sagging lodges and moved a few miles upstream to a fresh stand of trees.

The yearly calendar revolved around raising vegetables and hunting buffalo. The Pawnee planted corn and other crops in early May—about one acre for a family of four. In late June, when stalks stood high and were tough enough to withstand rabbits and other pests, most of the village emptied out for the first of the two annual buffalo hunts. Only the disabled, the very old, and the very young remained at home. Everyone else broke up into bands of about 25 people each that would trek the grasslands for several weeks, living in tipis, and carrying their provisions on the dog-drawn travois like the hunters farther west.

These part-time nomads returned by early August to begin the corn harvest. Saving the best kernels for seed, the women shucked, shelled,

Hewing to tradition in the era of the horse and wagon, a Sioux woman transports household goods on her dog-drawn travois, a device consisting of two poles framing a central platform. Migratory Plains peoples continued to use the dog-drawn travois for lighter loads even after horses became commonplace.

and stored the corn, and gathered wild plums, berries, and nuts. Meanwhile, the men hunted deer and antelope. In October everyone returned to the buffalo range for the autumn hunt aimed at procuring enough meat for the coming winter. The Pawnee prospered in their new homeland, growing in such numbers that, during the following three centuries, their earthen lodge villages spread as far west as the foothills of the Rockies.

Meanwhile, during the 14th century, another group of Caddoan speakers had left Texas. This tribe, later known as the Wichita, traveled only as far north as the Arkansas River in Kansas. Although their villages stood more than 200 miles southwest of the Pawnee settlements, the Wichita way of life paralleled that of their Caddoan-speaking cousins in most respects. One minor difference was that the Wichita covered their lodges with a thatch of long reeds and grasses, instead of earthen sod, so that they resembled haystacks. In adjusting to their new habitat, with its dual possibilities of corn and the buffalo, the Wichita and other tribes to come embraced many of the same ways.

During this period, tribes from a different language group began moving onto the edge of the Plains from the east and adopting the hunting-farming economy. They belonged to the Siouan-speaking family, which would eventually people the Plains with more than a dozen tribes and account for about half of the region's population. The Siouan speakers may have originated in the southeastern part of the continent and then, in about the 14th century, moved north into the Ohio Valley to raise corn amid the remnants of the fading Hopewell culture of mound builders. Sometime during the 15th century, the pressures of overpopulation evidently pushed the Siouan speakers westward. The first group to leave were the Hidatsa, who moved by stages westward across the Mississippi, then north along the Minnesota River. They found homes beyond the present Canadian border, in the Red River Valley of southern Manitoba.

En route westward, the Hidatsa had been harried from behind by the second group of Siouan-speaking people to depart the present-day Ohio-Indiana region, a loose confederation of bands who before their dispersal onto the Plains referred to themselves as Oceti Sakowin, or the "Seven Council Fires." The Oceti Sakowin settled down in the lake country of Wisconsin and Minnesota. They built substantial rectangular houses with heavy timber frames covered with large slabs of bark. Small herds of buffalo inhabited the meadows and prairies scattered among the forests and lakes and the open plains to the west.

These Indians hunted deer, elk, and bear, and the western bands hunted buffalo. But unlike the other Siouan speakers, they did not take up farming to any extent. Instead, they harvested wild rice. In late summer, the women paddled canoes into the swamps where large amounts of the grain thrived and, bending the stalks over their canoes, threshed it with their wooden paddles. Their new neighbors, the Ojibwa, also known as the Chippewa, called all of the Oceti Sakowin groups Nadowe-is-iw-ug, or "Lesser Adders," to contrast them with the hated Iroquois, whom the Ojibwa referred to as the "True Adders." The French pronounced the word *Nadouessioux*—and later abbreviated it to Sioux—the term the white Europeans used for all of the original Oceti Sakowin bands.

The next large group of Siouan speakers to leave the Ohio Valley were the Mandan. After crossing the Mississippi River, they built a complex of shelters made of thick layers of sod and earth over heavy log frames, much like those of the Pawnee. Like the Pawnee structures, these homes collapsed every decade or so, forcing the Mandan farther westward until they reached the Missouri at the junction of the White River. Over the years, always in search of new timber, the tribe moved up the Missouri. By the mid-1400s, they had found enough to satisfy their needs for centuries to come in the area of present-day Bismarck, North Dakota.

While Siouan- and Caddoan-speaking tribes were putting down roots as hunter-farmers on the eastern Plains, other migrants were moving in from the north. The Apache, whose name would one day be anathema to the U.S. Army, made the longest trek. Members of the Athapaskan language family whose ancestors had arrived in Alaska and Canada from northeastern Asia, the Apache began migrating southward in small bands early in the 14th century, about the same time that the Wichita started northward from Texas. They were nomadic hunters, and the game got bigger and better as they advanced onto the northern reaches of the Plains in Alberta. But the Apache kept going, pushing southeastward through present-day Montana and then down across the Platte River in Nebraska, passing west of the newly established Pawnee settlements. Farther south, in the Texas Panhandle, they finally found a land to their liking. For about nine months of the year, these Plains newcomers followed the buffalo herds. During the wintertime, they trekked westward into what is now New Mexico to camp near the Pueblo Indian villages along the Pecos River and to trade dried meat and hides for corn, squash, and cotton cloth.

THE LEGACY OF THE SEVEN COUNCIL FIRES

The people now known as the Sioux originally called themselves Oceti Sakowin—the Seven Council Fires. For them, as for many other Indians, a council fire was a symbol for a community. Although little is known of their history, the Seven Council Fires were evidently a loose federation of distinct groups. In the 1600s, however, whites entering their homeland around the upper Mississippi River began calling them all Sioux, derived from an Ojibwa term for a kind of snake.

Pressed by the Ojibwa, some of the Sioux peoples moved westward onto the Plains while others migrated southward. The four groups that stayed in the east spoke the Dakota dialect and emerged as the Santee, or Eastern Sioux. Two groups that reached the edge of the Plains spoke the Nakota dialect and formed the Middle Sioux. The far-ranging Western Sioux—also called the Teton or the Lakota, for their dialect—were a diverse group that associated as seven bands, or council fires, preserving the tradition.

SIOUX
Oceti Sakowin
(The Seven Council Fires)

TITONWAN / TETON (WESTERN)	WICIYELA (MIDDLE)	ISANTI / SANTEE (EASTERN)
LAKOTA	**NAKOTA**	**DAKOTA**
OGLALA *Scatter their Own*	IHANKTONWAN (YANKTON) *Dwellers at the End*	MDEWAKANTONWAN *Dwellers by the Sacred Lake*
SICANGU (BRULE) *Burnt Thigh*	IHANKTONWANNA (YANKTONAI) *Little Dwellers at the End*	WACHPEKUTE *Leaf Shooters*
MINICONJOU *Planters by the River*		WACHPETONWAN *Dwellers among the Leaves*
HUNKPAPA *Those Living at Entrance of Camp Circle*		SISITONWAN *People of the Marsh*
ITAZIPCO (SANS ARC) *No Bows*		
OOHENUNPA *Two Kettle*		
SIHASAPA *Blackfeet*		

Here, during the 16th century, the Apache became the first Plains people to encounter the Europeans. They had heard about the arrival of the Spanish explorers from their Pueblo contacts. Thus, in 1541, when the expedition of Francisco Vásquez de Coronado reached their encampment east of the Pecos, the Apache were far less surprised than the Spaniards. Coronado's scribe, Pedro de Castañeda, expressed astonishment at these strange people who "neither plant nor harvest maize" but "subsist entirely on cattle" (buffalo), "load their dogs like beasts of burden," and "have no permanent residence anywhere." Grasping for similarities, Coronado's men likened the Apache to the Bedouins.

This group of Apaches was only the vanguard of their people. Other Apache migrations followed the trail southward through Alberta. Eventually, the Apache fragmented into 10 or more distinct groups, dispersed over a broad expanse of prairie, mountain, and desert that reached from Arizona to Kansas. One group stopped in western Montana and struck up an alliance with a completely separate tribe, the Kiowa, longtime occupants of the Plains who spoke a language similar to that of the Pueblo Indians of the Rio Grande region. These Apaches became known as the Kiowa Apache. Another group, the Gataka Apache, veered off into the Black Hills of South Dakota.

The migration south of still another band of Apaches took a strange turn. This group stumbled on the westernmost outposts of the Pawnee along the South Platte River in northeastern Colorado. They pushed the Pawnee back into Nebraska before continuing south. But the Apache evidently took some of the Pawnee women captive and learned from them the secrets of building log and sod shelters and of growing corn. Reaching an area laced with small streams along the Colorado-Kansas border, the Apache built some Pawnee-style lodges and began to cultivate fields. In contrast to the Caddoan- and Siouan-speaking farmers of the eastern Plains who became ever more dependent on the buffalo, these migrants changed from being full-time nomadic hunters to part-time agriculturists.

On their way south through Canada, each wave of Apache peoples had passed through the rich hunting range of Alberta, but they paused only briefly. A longer stay was in all likelihood discouraged by the presence of a group of nomads who would grow in power on the Plains second only to the Sioux. They were the Nitzitapi, or "Blackfoot Confederacy," consisting of five Algonquian-speaking bands—the Blackfeet, the North and South Piegan, the Blood, and the Small Robes—with customs as well as language in common. Collectively, the members of the confederacy were called Blackfeet by the white Europeans who first encountered them. The name referred to the color of their moccasins, which presumably were either painted black or darkened with the charred remains of prairie fires.

No one knows how long the Blackfeet had pursued the buffalo in these far northern Plains. There were other Algonquian-speaking tribes stretched eastward through Canada and down the eastern coast of the North American continent. But the Blackfeet tongue varies so sharply from other Algonquian languages that it suggests an ancient separation from those peoples. The ancestors of the Blackfeet probably hunted the northern Plains for many centuries and may well have been the first people to make use of the jump-kill site known as Head-Smashed-In some 5,600 years ago.

The Blackfeet had no neighbors to their east until about the 17th century. At that time, another group of Algonquian speakers, the Arapaho, began moving southwestward from their ancestral homes located in the woodlands of Saskatchewan, near Lake Winnipeg. As the Arapaho traveled south, bound for the region between the North Platte and Arkansas rivers in present-day Wyoming and Colorado, a portion of the tribe split off.

Although most Indian men who rode the Plains favored simple gear, women such as these two Blackfeet often had richly decorated mounts. A favored accouterment was the crupper (above), an apronlike device that draped over the horse's hindquarters.

This splinter group would subsequently be labeled the Gros Ventre, or "Big Bellies," by French traders in a corruption of the Blackfeet term for them, Atsina, or "Gut People." The Gros Ventre demonstrated such a knack for getting along with the Blackfeet—in marked contrast to the Blackfeet neighbors to the west, the Shoshone and Kootenay, who periodically ventured out of the Rocky Mountains to hunt buffalo on the Plains—that they informally affiliated with the confederacy.

Until 1650 or so, the peopling of the Plains had proceeded at a leisurely pace. But during the late 17th century, new forces unleashed by the presence of Europeans came into play, sharply accelerating migrations onto the Plains. The first major instrument of change was the gun. Dutch, English, and French settlers along the eastern seaboard swapped firearms to Indians for furs, and soon tribes all along the colonial frontier clamored for the new weapons. Typically, the Indians turned the guns against their enemies to the west, touching off a series of shock waves that rippled through the Ohio and Mississippi valleys and onto the Plains. The most powerful of the newly armed groups was the Iroquois League. During the latter half of the 1600s, the Iroquois rampaged as far west as the Mississippi, disrupting the status quo among the tribes living around the Great Lakes. Although the Iroquois were eventually repulsed, local tribes such as the Mesquakie, the Cree, and the Ojibwa were supplied with firearms as a result of the Anglo-French rivalry for control of the western fur trade.

The beaded saddle below is typical of the handiwork of Crow women, noted for their finely wrought riding gear. The Crow also produced elegant quirts (above), similar to riding crops. A warrior used the rawhide lash of the quirt to urge on his horse—and sometimes to strike enemies in battle.

The guns in the hands of various groups of Native Americans who were reacting to the Iroquois onslaught reshaped the Siouan-speaking population of the Ohio Valley, which already had furnished at least two waves of migrants onto the Plains. The Hidatsa, the Sioux, and the Mandan had long since departed for the Plains; three other local Siouan-speaking tribes—the Iowa, the Oto, and the Ponca—had moved westward into the northeastern part of Iowa. Now, in the face of dislocations caused by Iroquois attacks on their eastern neighbors, the Osage, the Missouri, the Kansa, and the Omaha evacuated their farming villages along the banks of the Wabash River in Indiana.

All of these tribes crossed the Mississippi. The Osage built their villages along the present-day Missouri-Kansas-Oklahoma border, and the Missouri settled 300 miles to the north. The Kansa went up the Missouri River to the section of the Kansas River that is located in the state that eventually would be named for them, and then a few miles westward, winding up about 100 miles southeast of the Pawnee.

As for the Omaha, they had an unusual group of traveling companions on their trek westward. They were accompanied by a band of Caddoan speakers known as the Skidi Pawnee. Four centuries earlier, the Skidi Pawnee had separated from their close

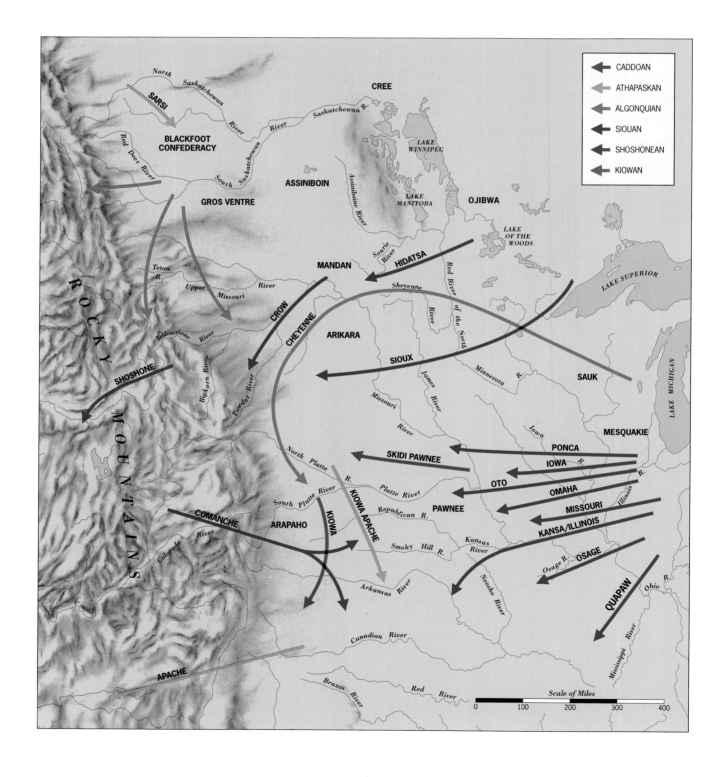

CADDOAN

ATHAPASKAN

ALGONQUIAN

SIOUAN

SHOSHONEAN

KIOWAN

CREE

SARSI

BLACKFOOT
CONFEDERACY

North *Saskatchewan* *River*

Red Deer River

South *Saskatchewan* *River*

Saskatchewan *River*

Saskatchewan R.

LAKE
WINNIPEG

ASSINIBOIN

GROS VENTRE

Assiniboine River

LAKE
MANITOBA

OJIBWA

LAKE
OF THE
WOODS

Teton R.

Upper

Missouri

River

MANDAN

Souris River

HIDATSA

LAKE SUPERIOR

Sheyenne

CROW

Yellowstone River

CHEYENNE

ARIKARA

River

Red River of the North

SHOSHONE

Bighorn River

Powder River

SIOUX

James River

Minnesota R.

SAUK

LAKE MICHIGAN

Missouri

River

MESQUAKIE

Iowa R.

PONCA

North Platte

SKIDI PAWNEE

IOWA

South Platte River

R.

Platte River

OTO

OMAHA

Illinois R.

ROCKY

COMANCHE

ARAPAHO

KIOWA

KIOWA
APACHE

Republican R.

PAWNEE

MISSOURI

KANSA/ILLINOIS

Colorado

River

Smoky *Hill R.*

Kansas *River*

Osage R. OSAGE

Neosho River

Arkansas River

MOUNTAINS

QUAPAW

Ohio *R.*

Mississippi River

APACHE

Canadian River

Brazos River

Red *River*

Scale of Miles

0   100   200   300   400

The arrival of Europeans in the New World stirred a second wave of migration onto the Great Plains starting in the late 17th century. White traders introduced firearms to assertive eastern groups such as the Iroquois, who then forced tribes to their west—including the Osage, Omaha, and Missouri—out onto the prairie. About the same time, tribes that had long dwelt in the Rockies and Great Basin, such as the Comanche, acquired horses and swept onto the grasslands to hunt buffalo and raid rival groups.

relatives in east Texas and drifted northeastward into the Ohio Valley. Fleeing the disruptions caused by the Iroquois and the Anglo-French wars, they had joined up with the Omaha. But when the Omaha stopped in Iowa, the Skidi Pawnee continued traveling westward. Upon reaching the Platte River, they discovered the old pioneers in these parts, the Pawnee, and reunited with their former brethren. Like the Siouan-speaking tribes in this latest migration onto the Plains, they adopted the Pawnee way of life, combining buffalo hunting with farming.

Farther north during the 17th century, firearms were also exerting a profound effect on the Siouan-speaking migrants from the Ohio Valley. Up in the Red River Valley of southern Manitoba, the Hidatsa came under attack after three peaceful centuries of farming and hunting. Their assailants were the Cree and the Ojibwa. Both were Algonquian-speaking tribes trying to expand their beaver-trapping territories beyond the forests near Lake Superior, with the aid of guns supplied by French fur traders operating out of Montreal. The Cree and the Ojibwa eventually forced the Hidatsa to abandon their homes.

Fleeing to the southwest, the Hidatsa settled on the Missouri River near its confluence with the Heart River in the middle of what is now North Dakota. An outbreak of smallpox in 1781 forced them to resettle to the south along the Knife River. They built their dome-shaped earthen lodges just a few miles north of the Mandan villages, and with the help of seed corn provided by their Siouan-speaking cousins, succeeded again as farmers and hunters. Parts of the tribe broke away over the years and migrated westward, up the Missouri and Yellowstone rivers. They gradually gave up agriculture altogether to hunt the buffalo of southern Montana and northern Wyoming. Members of these splinter groups referred to themselves as Absaroka. The word means a "large bird"; since early French explorers assumed the bird was a crow, these Hidatsa descendants became known by the whites as the Crow.

To the east in the central Minnesota lake country, other Siouan speakers also came under pressure from the Ojibwa and the Cree. These were the Indians who had migrated from the Ohio Valley to the headwaters of the Mississippi. Even before the attacks, this loose confederation was fragmenting into a profusion of smaller communities. The first tribe to split away were the Assiniboin, who may have separated as early as 1600 and then drifted northwestward into Manitoba, where they became bitter enemies of the Sioux. Other Sioux, who came to be known as the Teton, moved westward toward the Missouri. With the help of the Cree, the Ojibwa drove the Sioux closer to the open prairies, thus accelerating the trend toward increased buffalo hunting.

The introduction of guns in the region generated a ripple effect. As the Ojibwa shoved the Sioux westward, they in turn dislodged a group of Algonquian speakers living along the Minnesota River near the border with South Dakota. This tribe, the Cheyenne, already had been displaced from their ancestral land near the Great Lakes by the chain reaction that had been set in motion in the east by the arming of the Iroquois. Now, early in the 18th century, they moved westward again and settled along the Cheyenne River in North Dakota. Among the settlements they constructed, one large village contained at least 70 circular earthen lodges and was guarded by a deep ditch and palisaded wall overlooking the bottom lands where the Cheyenne grew corn, beans, and squash.

The impressive Cheyenne settlement was short lived. Their fortified village soon came under challenge from a plethora of raiders. According to various tribal histories, the Cheyenne were attacked by all four adversaries in the region: the Sioux, the Cree, the Ojibwa, and the Assiniboin. One morning about 50 years after the village was built, an Ojibwa war party hid in the woods close to the Cheyenne settlement. As soon as the Cheyenne men left to hunt buffalo, the Ojibwa stormed the village, killed or captured most of the women and children, and set the lodges ablaze. The disheartened remnants of the Cheyenne had to move again westward, some 150 miles to the Missouri River.

But the Cheyenne did not remain long here either, probably because of renewed pressure from the Sioux. By the first decade of the 18th century, they were across the Missouri and into the Black Hills of South Dakota. There they joined up with the Suhtaio, members of their tribe who had left them many decades before in Minnesota to strike out westward. The reunited Cheyenne now abandoned farming—"lost the corn," as their oral tradition puts it—and began to hunt the buffalo year-round. It was not the gun alone that had driven them onto the Plains as full-time nomads but the acquisition of another European resource—the horse.

Although the Spanish explorer Coronado had brought horses onto the Plains in 1541, more than 15,000 years after the extinction of the native species, nearly a century and a half passed before the Indians acquired them in numbers. Spanish officials in the New Mexico colony forbade the

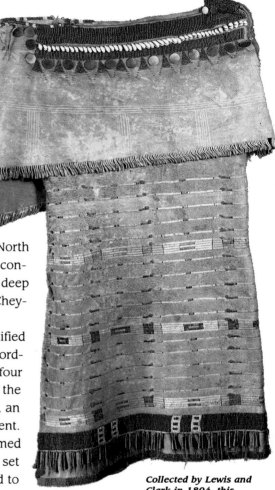

Collected by Lewis and Clark in 1804, this northern Plains dress, adorned with beads and porcupine quills, was fashioned from a single moose hide, folded along one flank and sewn on the other. The top was doubled over to form a bodice, with armholes that were made by cutting the folded side and leaving the other side open.

trading of either horses or guns to native peoples. They did hire local Pueblo Indians to work with the animals, however, and a few strays or stolen mounts eventually found their way into Indian hands. Then, in 1680, a revolt by the Pueblos drove the Spaniards out of the region temporarily, leaving large herds available for rounding up.

Among the earliest groups to take advantage of this windfall were the Apache farmers living in the Arkansas Valley. They traded regularly with the Pueblos and, as a result of these connections, were able to acquire both horses and equestrian know-how. The Apache also became renowned as horse thieves, marauding south of the Rio Grande to raid Spanish ranches. Through a combination of stealing and intertribal trading, the Indians dispersed horses across the length and breadth of the Plains with extraordinary speed. By 1700 the Pawnee and the Wichita had them. By 1750 the Blackfeet in Alberta were fully mounted. By about 1770, the horse had reached the Sioux in western Minnesota.

Plains Indians took to horses with such ease that the white people who witnessed their expert horsemanship swore that they must have been riding for centuries. Indian riders borrowed their early equipment from the Spaniards, but they enlivened it with their own colorful and spiritually charged trappings, including eagle feathers, symbolic markings, and human scalps.

The horse transformed Plains nomadism from a life of subsistence into one of abundance. Hunters could now pursue the buffalo much farther and faster than was ever possible on foot. They were capable of following the herds for scores of miles at almost any time of year, and the best of their horses could outrun even a stampeding buffalo. In a single day, it was possible for two or three mounted hunters to kill enough buffalo to provide 10 pounds of fresh meat daily for each member of a band of 100 persons for a week.

The horse was also a far more efficient beast of burden than the dog. It could pull a travois laden with 300 pounds about 40 miles a day, or twice as far as the maximum distance a dog could haul a load one-fourth as heavy. The Indians could now carry larger reserves of food, amass more possessions, and sew larger tipis. Some tribes referred to the horse's abilities as a pack animal with wonder, calling it "mystery dog," "medicine dog," or "sacred dog." The Blackfeet simply called the horse "big dog." As an additional bonus, the horse was herbivorous and grazed on the abundant prairie grass.

A Comanche dress of the late 1800s, fringed with rawhide tassels and painted in the manner characteristic of the tribe, consists of three skins, two forming the skirt and one the blouse. The use of two or more smaller hides for dressmaking became increasingly common on the Plains as the supply of large game animals dwindled.

The free life of the mounted nomad made village routine seem tame in comparison. The ready supply of fresh buffalo meat throughout the year was a potent attraction. It was not only the Cheyenne who gave up farming and their earthen lodges to follow the buffalo. Other former villagers—among them the Crow, the Arapaho, and several groups of the Sioux—also took up the nomadic life, joining the ranks of other full-time hunters like the Blackfeet, the Assiniboin, the Comanche, the Cree, and the Kiowa. Even those tribes that stayed with their villages, such as the Pawnee, the Mandan, the Hidatsa, and the Arikara, extended the length of their twice-a-year forays in quest of the buffalo.

No tribe's way of life was more dramatically reshaped by the horse than that of the Comanche, a group with no previous connection to the Plains. Before 1700 the Comanche were an impoverished Shoshonean-speaking group of hunter-gatherers living in the mountains of western Colorado. Then they acquired horses. Mounted Comanches descended from the Rockies, rapidly evolving as superb horsemen and buffalo hunters. The Comanche, a white plainsman said, believed that "the Great Spirit had created horses especially for them."

They swept down upon various Apache bands, including those in northern Texas. These Apaches, after nearly three centuries of residence, were driven westward across the mountains into Arizona and New Mexico. By the 1760s, the Comanche ruled the southern Plains from central Kansas into Texas and dispatched their own raiding parties into Mexico to secure additional horses.

This Sioux dress, crafted in the 1880s from two deerskins joined at the sides, exemplifies the elaborate and painstaking beadwork favored by that culture's craftswomen.

In the northern Plains, the combination of horse and gun led to ever-changing patterns of migration and territorial control. The horse stimulated intertribal warfare both as an object of wealth—stealing another tribe's horses became an honorable activity—and as an instrument of war that enabled warriors to attack enemies too far away to reach on foot. And by bringing more people onto the Plains and expanding their hunting range, the horse contributed to friction over control of the best hunting grounds. The horse's efficiency also provided more leisure time, much of which was consumed by planning, making, and celebrating warfare.

In the northeast Plains, the Cheyenne and the Sioux emerged as dom-

A three-skin Cheyenne dress made in 1890 is lavishly decorated with cowrie shells obtained in trade from distant tribes living near warm ocean waters.

inant powers. After their advance across the Missouri and into the Black Hills in the early 1700s, the Cheyenne displaced the Kiowa, the Kiowa Apache, and the Gataka Apache, who moved south into Colorado and Nebraska. Gaining a reputation for warlike ferocity that belied their small numbers, the Cheyenne ranged westward to challenge the Crow in Wyoming and Montana and southward into Nebraska to fight the Pawnee.

In the meantime, the Sioux were remaking the map of the northern Plains, largely through the efforts of the seven subgroups of the Teton wing of the tribe. After having pushed the Cheyenne westward during the 18th century, the Teton Sioux adopted the horse in force and, in 1792, drove the Arikara, who had been badly weakened by the smallpox epidemic in 1780, from their villages on the Missouri. Then the Teton crossed the Missouri River and attacked the Cheyenne again in the Black Hills. Before long, the Teton claimed all of the Dakotas as their hunting grounds and, like the Cheyenne, encroached on the territory of the Crow.

To the northwest, the Blackfoot Confederacy blossomed as the predominant power. Growing strong on the abundant buffalo herds of Alberta and Saskatchewan, its tribes increased in population. In 1780 the year before a smallpox epidemic reduced their numbers by about one-third, there were an estimated 10,000 Blackfeet, whose confederacy ranked second in size only to the Sioux among all of the Plains Indians.

The Blackfeet, moreover, could call on the help of two neighboring tribes. In addition to the Gros Ventre, a second group of allies had appeared in the region. These were the Sarsi, a small tribe of perhaps fewer than 1,000 persons who came down from the woodlands farther north late in the 17th century. They were the last tribe to migrate onto the Plains and the last group of Athapaskan peoples whose southward exodus from Alaska and northern Canada had begun with the Apache three centuries earlier. Confronted by overwhelming Blackfeet superiority, the Sarsi in effect joined up. They adopted so many Blackfeet customs that, despite their disparate language and background, white people would frequently mistake them for their powerful neighbors.

GARDENS OF THE HIDATSA

Unlike other peoples of the Plains who abandoned the settled life for a nomadic existence once they had horses, the Hidatsa of present-day North Dakota clung to their villages along the Missouri River, living in earth lodges and cultivating the rich alluvial soil. In spring and summer, while the men of the tribe ventured out to hunt, the women tended their gardens. Using tools and techniques dating as far back as AD 1100, they raised corn—the tribe's staple—along with squash, beans, and sunflowers, and preserved much of the harvest to see their families through the hard winter ahead.

The proud horticultural tradition cherished by the Hidatsa peoples was epitomized by Buffalo Bird Woman *(right),* an accomplished gardener and artisan who was born about 1840 and learned the secrets of working the soil from her elder kinswomen in the village of Like-a-fishhook, located on a sharp bend in the Missouri River. Late in life, Buffalo Bird Woman shared her accumulated Hidatsa lore with anthropologist Gilbert Wilson, who faithfully recorded her observations.

The planting season at Like-a-fishhook began as the winter's snow melted, when members of the Goose Society—a women's organization dedicated to watching over the gardens and ensuring their fertility—welcomed the spirits of growth and greenery back from the south with dance and ceremonies. The women then cleared away dead leaves with special rakes tipped with deer antlers, favored by the Hidatsa long after iron tools became available from white traders. The first seeds sown were the sunflowers, which took the longest time to mature, followed by corn. "We Hidatsa women were early risers in the planting season," Buffalo Bird Woman recalled. "It was my habit to be up before sunrise."

The task demanded more than good tools and hard work, however. A successful gardener had to be truly devoted to her crops. "We thought the corn plants had souls," Buffalo Bird Woman explained. "We cared for our corn in those days, as we would care for a child." In keeping with that spirit, the women watched over their vulnerable charges from stages in the fields, shooing away crows and other pests and encouraging the plants with songs. "We thought that our growing corn liked to hear us sing," recounted Buffalo Bird Woman, "just as children like to hear their mother sing to them."

Buffalo Bird Woman, pictured here in 1910, came of age in the village of Like-a-fishhook (inset), a cluster of earth lodges surrounded by a palisade, from which women issued daily to tend plots in the bottom lands.

A woman seated on a stage amid the ripening corn minds her young children while guarding the plants against the age-old threats—birds, horses, and mischievous boys.

A gardener works the soil with a traditional hoe like the one displayed, made from the shoulder bone of a buffalo fixed to a wooden handle. Before hoeing, a woman cleared her plot with an antler rake (bottom), evoking the legend of Everlasting Grandmother, whose fields were raked by deer using their horns.

Braids of seed corn hang from a platform to dry at Fort Berthold. Seed corn was stored in braided form until it was ready for planting, at which time the kernels were removed by hand. The other ears were dried on the floor of the platform and then released into a threshing booth below (inset), where the kernels were knocked loose with sticks.

In a photograph taken about 1916, a Hidatsa woman uses a knife made from a buffalo's shoulder bone to pare squash. Such bone knives (inset) were used "for slicing squash and nothing else," Buffalo Bird Woman recalled. Afterward, the slices of squash were strung on wooden spits to dry.

A HARVEST ABOUNDING

When the corn ripened, Hidatsa women picked the ears and heaped them up for husking by the men, who were rewarded with a feast. Afterward, the women carried the harvest home, a task later eased by horses and wagons. The best ears were set aside and braided together, using the thin inner leaves that still adhered to the stem. Those braids were then dried on platforms to provide seeds for planting. Finally, the braided seed corn was stored with other dried crops in underground caches.

This routine was disrupted in 1882 when Buffalo Bird Woman and her fellow villagers were resettled on family lots at the Fort Berthold Reservation. There, officials introduced the Hidatsa to strange new crops and encouraged the men to become farmers, depriving women of their central role. Yet certain traditions persisted. Buffalo Bird Woman still tended a garden, and in 1911, the corn she raised won first prize at a reservation fair. She credited her success to the old ways. "I rise at daybreak and steal out to the cornfields," she confided, "and as I hoe the corn I sing to it, as we did when I was young."

Dried crops were stored in underground pits like the one at far right, dug by Buffalo Bird Woman along the Missouri River in 1912 to demonstrate how the pits were made in the old days. The accompanying diagram shows the pit's grass lining, which kept the contents dry, and the placement of the crops—the perishable squash at center, surrounded by shelled corn and braided seed corn.

Given the growing numerical strength of the Blackfeet, it took only the acquisition of the horse and the gun to galvanize their tendencies toward expansion. About 1785 they began to extend their hunting territory southward into Montana and took on old enemies. In less than 20 years, Blackfeet warriors shoved the Flathead and the Kootenay back into the mountains and dispossessed the Shoshone. Blackfeet raiding parties in search of horses sometimes ranged far beyond the confederacy's newly expanded hunting grounds. They struck eastward into the prized herds of the Crow and more than 1,000 miles southward to the Rio Grande, gaining the tribe further notoriety.

While former farmers like the Cheyenne and the Teton Sioux quickly gravitated to the nomadic life on horseback, other tribes clung to their traditional ways. There was no lack of horses. Such longtime village dwellers as the Pawnee, the Wichita, the Omaha, and the Mandan were well supplied with mounts relatively early in the century, yet they remained sedentary. Even a large number of Sioux stayed behind in the Minnesota lake country to gather wild rice, farm, and periodically hunt buffalo. This branch, known as the Santee, numbered as many as 12,000 in 1782, about half of the Sioux population. The Santee would hold out here until 1862 when the United States government ordered them dispersed to reservations in southern Minnesota and the Dakota Territory.

Vast improvements in the productivity of their crops kept many of these tribes anchored to their old lands. Along the upper Missouri, the women, who did most of the farming, had developed frost- and drought-resistant varieties of corn, squash, beans, and sunflowers that were especially well adapted to the short northern growing season. The Hidatsa grew five types of beans and no fewer than nine varieties of corn. In Minnesota, the Santee Sioux learned to grow corn so efficiently that they could harvest a yield of more than 25 bushels per acre in a good season.

The surplus crops, in turn, attracted the nomadic tribes and transformed the farming villages into flourishing centers of trade. Cheyenne, Sioux, and Assiniboin would ride into Mandan and Hidatsa settlements to barter dried meat, buffalo hides, and turkey tail feathers for corn and squash. Horses also changed hands, along with other imports such as guns, ammunition, metal utensils, and European cloth that filtered down the trade networks from French and English outposts in Canada.

The Mandan and the Hidatsa were shrewd traders. They sometimes passed along horses and guns to the nomadic tribes at a markup of 100 percent. During much of the 18th century, the two tribes lived only about

20 miles apart in clusters of populous villages that may have consisted of as many as two dozen earth lodges and housed up to 1,000 residents each. Their combined population probably numbered about 11,500. But the two tribes were in constant danger from nomads who periodically swept in to take what they wanted without the niceties of trade. The locals fortified their villages, erecting wooden palisades and ringing their settlements with ditches. The Hidatsa had a rule, however, that no outsider who came to trade could be harmed while inside the village.

The villagers shared in the great flowering of the Plains culture about the turn of the 19th century. Indeed, some of these tribes may well have been responsible for contributing such cultural innovations as the elaborate religious ceremonies that white men would call the Sun Dance and the concept of an internal police force—the so-called Dog Soldiers who enforced discipline during the communal hunt. But the glamour and glory belonged to the nomads, those mounted hunter-warriors who reveled in the chase after the buffalo and the charge against the enemy. It was those tribes who would so impress the intruding white men as both fearsome and noble, as free as the fierce winds whipping across the vast Plains.

While the introduction of the horse and gun helped usher in the golden era of the Plains Indians, the actual presence of white men brought mixed blessings. Traders—French from Saint Louis, and French and British from Canada—had been visiting the eastern villages since the early 1700s to obtain beaver, wolf, raccoon, and other furs. But the federal government expedition by Meriwether Lewis and William Clark up the Missouri River and westward to the Pacific, completed in 1806, triggered a flurry of interest by American trappers and traders. Permanent trading centers sprang up on the Plains, including a post in the heart of Crow country at the mouth of the Bighorn River. The posts began specializing in buffalo products, such as tallow for candles and soap, and buffalo robes—hides tanned with the hair still on, which were popular as blankets and floor coverings.

One of the groups in the best position to profit from the buffalo trade were those formidable custodians of the northwest Plains, the Blackfeet. The Blackfeet had the largest supply of buffalo hides handy to river transportation, the easiest way to move the bulky items. But for more than two decades, they zealously resisted the efforts of both British and American companies to establish trading centers in Montana. Fearing that the pres-

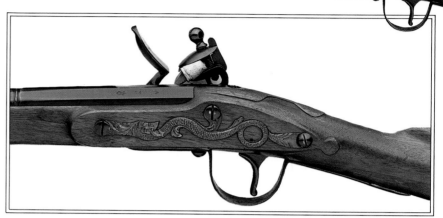

Plains Indians called trade muskets like this 19th-century model "golden serpents" because of the brass emblem on the side plate (inset). Although the Indians considered the emblem a mark of quality, it was sometimes affixed to inferior weapons.

Comanche Indians exchanged hides and furs for luxury items like this decorative European mirror dating from the 1860s, which was found near Palo Duro Canyon in the Texas Panhandle.

ence of white men would result in delivering firearms into the hands of their enemies, the Blackfeet burned trading posts and killed or drove away the unfortunate occupants. Not until 1832, with the erection of Fort McKenzie on the upper reaches of the Missouri, did they relent.

Other tribes were so eager to engage in trade that they abandoned old hunting grounds to move closer to the outposts. The establishment of Bent's Fort on the Arkansas River in southeast Colorado in 1833 lured the migration southward of about half of the Cheyenne from the Black Hills, leading to a permanent north-south split of that tribe. With their old comrades, the Arapaho, the Southern Cheyenne took control of the hunting grounds of west Kansas and much of eastern Colorado, once again dispossessing the Kiowa and the Kiowa Apache, who moved farther south. The next year, the construction of another trading post, Fort Laramie, on the North Platte River in southeastern Wyoming, attracted the Oglala branch of the Teton Sioux from their territory east of the Black Hills.

With trade came not only prosperity but also catastrophe. Trade networks involving whites carried their deadly bacteria and viruses as well as valued goods. Epidemics of cholera, measles, influenza, and smallpox periodically devastated the Indians, who had no immunity to such diseases. These epidemics were exacerbated by the refusal of the Indians to quarantine victims—isolating the sick and dying was spiritually alien to them—and by the unsanitary conditions in their camps. The nomadic bands normally handled the problem of disposing of refuse and sewage by moving every day or two. But once a disease like smallpox struck, movement became impossible, and contagious materials rapidly piled up.

What may have been the worst smallpox epidemic to ravage the Plains began in Texas at the Spanish settlement of San Antonio in 1780. Some Wichita Indians who visited the outpost once each year carried the virus back to their villages on the Red River. From there the disease

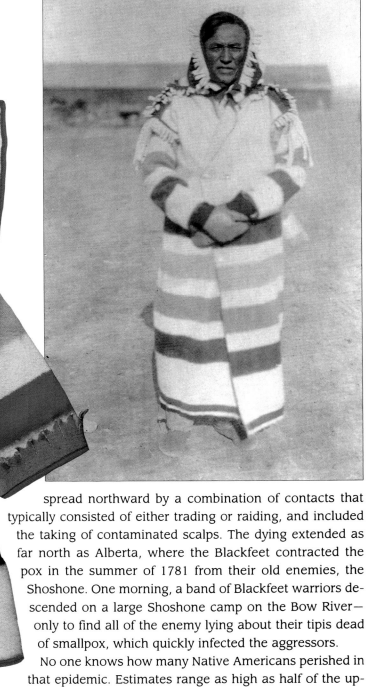

Among the white trade goods coveted by tribes on the northern Plains was the Hudson's Bay blanket, which replaced the buffalo robe as the preferred winter garment for some groups. The Blackfeet fashioned the blankets into capotes of the sort worn by the man below; the hooded garment (left) was made famous by French trappers.

spread northward by a combination of contacts that typically consisted of either trading or raiding, and included the taking of contaminated scalps. The dying extended as far north as Alberta, where the Blackfeet contracted the pox in the summer of 1781 from their old enemies, the Shoshone. One morning, a band of Blackfeet warriors descended on a large Shoshone camp on the Bow River—only to find all of the enemy lying about their tipis dead of smallpox, which quickly infected the aggressors.

No one knows how many Native Americans perished in that epidemic. Estimates range as high as half of the upper Plains' population of approximately 130,000. The toll in later epidemics was better documented, as increasing numbers of white traders were present to witness the awful effects of the scourges they inadvertently visited upon the Plains.

In June 1837, the steamers *St. Peter* and *Yellowstone* sailed up the Missouri to collect buffalo robes for a cargo that included guns, ammunition, and smallpox. From its beginnings with the infection of a single crew member, the epidemic soon blazed a trail of tragedy through the Mandan, the Hidatsa, and the Arikara and then into the trading posts erected near nomadic tribes, including Fort Union on the Missouri. As many as 10,000 Indians died in just a few weeks. Some 4,000 of the 8,000 Assiniboins were wiped out; survivors insisted on peddling all their robes at Fort Union that awful summer despite the danger of infection because they said they would have no need of them if they died before winter.

A keelboat from Fort Union bore the scourge upstream to Fort McKenzie. Despite efforts on the part of the traders to keep the Blackfeet away from the sick, the Indians swarmed over the post, eager to obtain guns and ammunition. Within four years, half of the confederacy's population of 15,000 lay dead of the pox. In one Piegan camp, the only survivors were two elderly women who had gained immunity as young girls by living through the 1781 epidemic.

The new epidemic rearranged the power structure of the Indian tribes on the northern Plains. In the deadly chain of infection, only the Sioux came out ahead. They incurred the disease while raiding the stricken villages of the upper Missouri and unwittingly passed it on to their hostile southern neighbors, the Pawnee—ironically via Sioux scalps that had been taken by the Pawnee. The Pawnee were so weakened by smallpox that they ceased to be a threat to Sioux hunting grounds. On the upper Missouri, meanwhile, the pox strengthened the position of the Sioux by reducing the once-powerful Mandan and Hidatsa to a single combined village. The Mandan population, decimated by the 1780 epidemic, shrank from more than 1,800 to 138 in a period of three months.

Now, with free rein along a 250-mile stretch of the river, the Sioux enjoyed an expanded dominance over a large portion of the northern Plains. The Blackfeet, on the other hand, fell upon humble times. With the ranks of their warriors depleted by the high death toll and the survivors tormented by the belief that the pox had struck because they had displeased the sacred powers, the Blackfeet relinquished some of their hunting grounds and withdrew back toward the Canadian border.

A Yankton Sioux winter count inscribed on a piece of cotton trade cloth records memorable events in the life of the people from 1823 to 1911, beginning with the earliest entry at the lower right corner and spiraling inward in a clockwise direction. Every winter the keepers of the count chose a pictograph to stand for the year—such as stars in the circle of the sky (lower left), representing the Leonid meteor shower of November 1833; spotted bodies (upper left), signifying the great smallpox epidemic of 1837 and 1838; and crossed muskets, representing tribal conflicts in later years. Starting in 1877, each entry features a log cabin to mark the transition to reservation life.

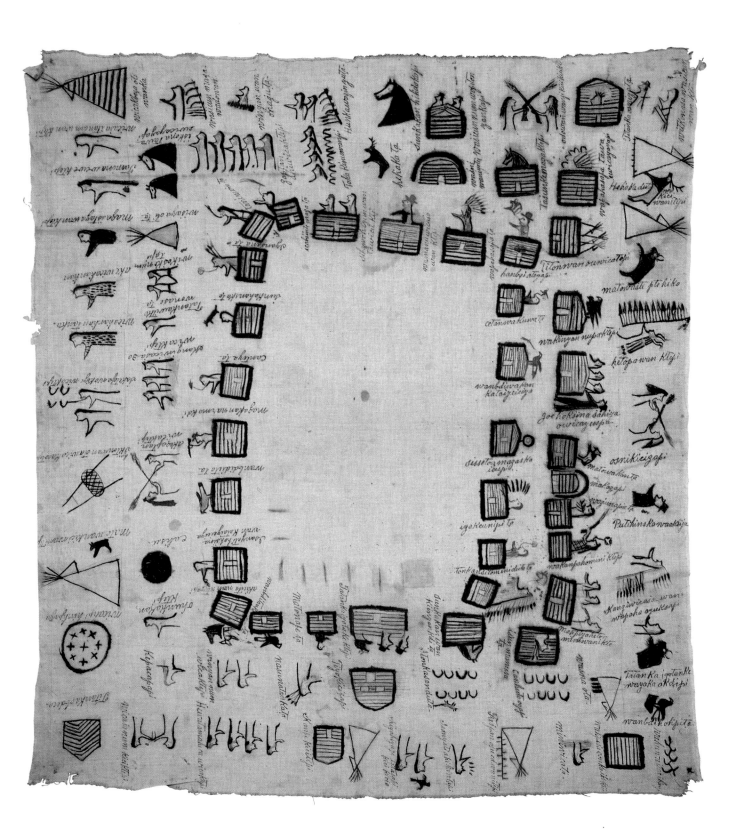

An even more virulent—and eventually decisive—threat to the Indian way of life came with the white invasion of the Plains. The opening of the Oregon Trail during the early 1840s brought trains of covered wagons rolling westward. In 1849, during a six-week period, some 40,000 settlers and fortune seekers in quest of California gold drove up the Platte River. En route, they killed off or scared away the buffalo, and their livestock ate up the grass, transforming the trail into a dusty wasteland several miles wide that divided the Plains and disrupted buffalo migration patterns.

Much of the initial contact was peaceable, with the Indians encouraging trade and charging nominal tolls for passing through their lands. Occasionally, however, roving war parties attacked the wagon trains, stealing livestock and killing whites. The United States government responded with small military expeditions, accelerating the conflict. To forestall the perceived danger to westward expansion, Washington convened a council of Plains tribes at Fort Laramie in the fall of 1851. Several of these tribes had treaties of friendship with the United States, dating back to 1825, but this was the first time the issue of territory was raised. Several thousand Indians attended, the majority of them Oglala Sioux, who claimed the hunting grounds around Fort Laramie, but also delegates from eight other tribes. In the council meetings, each tribe was asked to define the boundaries of its hunting grounds and to promise to remain within them. These designated territories, sanctioned by treaties signed during the council, became the basis for the later system of ever-shrinking reservations on which the tribes would be confined. In exchange, the federal government promised to distribute thousands of dollars' worth of trade goods annually.

The decisions at Fort Laramie effectively ended thousands of years of Indian migration on the Plains—but they did little to bring about peace. Washington's goal was to keep the westward trail open, not to establish accurate boundaries between the tribes, and some of the territories bore little resemblance to actual Indian holdings. In any event, the United States government would repeatedly violate these and other treaties by provoking nearly three decades of intermittent warfare with Plains tribes.

While the Indians struggled to stop the encroachments of the white man, another campaign that would undermine their way of life was increasing in intensity. By the 1860s, legions of professional hunters had begun stalking the buffalo. The building of the transcontinental railroad across the Plains created a demand for fresh buffalo meat to feed the construction crews. Once completed, the railroads provided cheap transportation to the East, where development of new commercial tanning techniques converted even the poorest buffalo hide into usable leather.

With processors paying as much as $3 for a single hide, hunters flocked to the Plains, and the hide market flourished. At the peak of the slaughter from 1872 through 1874, more than six million buffalo were slain in the southern Plains alone—80 percent of them at the hands of white hunters. Killing buffalo became such a popular pastime that the railroads even ran special excursion trains from which tourists could gun down the creatures through the open coach windows.

The United States government did nothing to stop the slaughter, even when the hunters poached on the Indian reservations. Officials in Washington coveted the Plains for white farmers and ranchers. Those who were planning the future of the West did not recognize a role for the Native Americans. One way or another, the Indians would be forced to stop hunting altogether and retire to the reservations to become Christianized farmers. As Secretary of the Interior Columbus Delano tersely put it in 1872: "It is our duty to coerce them, if necessary, into the adoption and practice of our habits and customs."

Killing off the buffalo was the simplest way to achieve these aims. General Philip Sheridan, a Union hero of the Civil War and one of the leading Indian fighters, made this explicit in 1875 when he successfully convinced the Texas legislature to defeat a measure that was intended to preserve the buffalo from extinction. The hide hunters, he declared, "have done more in the last two years to settle the vexed Indian question than the entire regular army has done in the past 30 years. They are destroying the Indians' commissary. For the sake of lasting peace, let them kill, skin, and sell until the buffaloes are exterminated."

The hunters came within a hairsbreadth of Sheridan's goal. The century that had begun with an estimated 60 million buffalo roaming the American range ended with only a few hundred remaining—and none of them running free. With the buffalo gone, the Plains tribes faced a terrible choice: starvation or a diminished existence within the confines of a reservation. While their communities endured, the age of the nomadic hunter had come to a tragic conclusion.

The plight of the Plains Indians was poignantly symbolized in 1913 when James Earle Fraser sought models for the commemorative nickel that he had been commissioned to design. He located his three Indian chiefs living on reservations established by the federal government. He found his buffalo in New York City, penned up in the Bronx Zoo.

THE SACRED HILLS

Described as the "heart of everything that is," the Black Hills straddling the border of South Dakota and Wyoming have long held great spiritual significance for the native peoples of the region. Among the world's oldest mountain ranges, the dark pine-forested bluffs rise from the enveloping prairie like mysterious islands in an ocean of grass. For centuries, Indians have climbed the craggy hills at right to commune with their spirits and seek guidance from visions. Indeed, for tribes of the area, the Black Hills remain the holiest of places, a wilderness shrine equally suffused with physical beauty and supernatural power.

The legends associated with the Black Hills and nearby features such as the Badlands express the conviction of Native Americans that the land has shaped their destiny. Both the Cheyenne and the Lakota Sioux say the region was once the site of a great and fateful contest. According to a legend of the Lakota, at one time there were no Black Hills interrupting the endless stretch of plains. In this chaotic world of long ago, humans and their fellow creatures preyed indiscriminately upon one another. To bring order to this realm, man summoned all the animals to a race. Following an enormous circular path outlined on the prairie, the creatures raced around and around in a mad frenzy. The tumult seemed to disturb the spirits, for soon the path sank beneath the racers' pounding feet, and the ground amid the circle rose up, forming a mountainous bulge that eventually burst and showered the creatures with debris. Many were killed, including the monsters called the Unkcheghila, whose huge bones can still be found in the area. Humans survived the holocaust, and claimed the right to prey on other animals. But the Black Hills standing at the site of the ancient cataclysm served as a reminder to the people that their strength was insignificant compared with the awesome power of the spirits abiding in the earth.

DEVILS TOWER

Looming above the Belle Fourche River in northeastern Wyoming, the great shaft of stone known as Devils Tower has long been associated by Plains Indians with the creature the Lakota call Mató, or the "Bear." According to the Kiowa, a spirit once appeared to a proud young girl in the form of a great bear and changed her into that same shape. Reveling in her new-found power, the giant bear girl chased after her seven siblings and threatened to devour them, until they jumped atop a low rock and prayed for help to the Great Spirit. At once the rock began to grow upward, elevating them beyond their sister's reach. Enraged, she leaped and clawed at the sides of the rock. But her siblings grew ever more distant, rising clear into the heavens, where they became the seven stars of the Pleiades. Left behind on the tower's walls were signs of the bear girl's thwarted fury—long claw marks engraved deep in the stone.

BEAR BUTTE

Protruding from the plains just east of the Black Hills proper is a lonely and majestic outcropping, dubbed Bear Butte by the Lakota. According to tribal legend, the butte was formed in ancient times as a result of a titanic struggle between a huge bear and a monstrous Unkcheghila. For days, the two giants clashed, shedding blood in streams, until at last the bear conceded defeat and went off on its own to die. When the bear collapsed, the earth convulsed and covered its body. All that remained was the massive mound. Atop this butte, some say the Lakota chief Crazy Horse received supernatural powers from the spirit of a bear. The Cheyenne, for their part, consider Bear Butte the most sacred place on earth. It was there that the Cheyenne prophet Sweet Medicine received the four Sacred Arrows that brought blessings to his people. To this day, the Cheyenne and Lakota make pilgrimages to Bear Butte to pray and fast.

HARNEY PEAK

*The granite summi
of Harney Peak,
highest of the Blac
Hills, was said to b
the nesting place o
a legendary creatu
long dreaded and
revered by the La-
kota—the frightful
Wakinyan, or
"Thunderbird."
Flashing lightning
from its eyes and
booming thunder
with each flap of it
wings, the great
bird brought down
violent storms, mo
ing even the boldes
of men to pray. El
ers warned young-
sters who went up
the mountain in
search of inspira-
tion not to go too
near the craggy
summit: "That is
the Wakinyan's
place. Do not tres-
pass on it." Yet on
privileged seeker,
the great Lakota
medicine man Bla
Elk, was taken to
the top of Harney
Peak by spirit guid
during a vision he
had at the age of
nine. There, the h
mountain was re-
vealed to him as t
center of the uni-
verse for his peopl*

BADLANDS

Sculpted by countless centuries of erosion into a haunting landscape of hills, canyons, and gullies, the desert region stretching east of the Black Hills is known to the Lakota as Makoshicha, or the "Badlands." Once covered by an inland sea and later roamed by dinosaurs, the Badlands and its fossil remains are associated in Lakota lore with the Unktehi, monsters inhabiting the primordial waters from which the earth emerged. According to one Lakota legend, long ago the Unktehi turned against the human race and began causing devastating floods, thus angering the Wakinyan, who worried that there would be no people left to pray to the Thunderbird and dream of its power. The Wakinyan sent down blazing thunderbolts that dried up the floodwaters and consumed the malicious Unktehi, whose bones still lie amid the tortured Badlands to remind people of the terror and wonder of the spirits.

WIND CAVE

Deep in a ravine at the southern edge of the Black Hills, where the forested slopes give way to the grasslands, lies the entrance to a cavern commonly known as Wind Cave (inset) but long revered by the Lakota as Washun Niya, or the "Breathing Hole." Named for the sighing sounds that emanate from it, the opening is just large enough for a person to pass through. In Lakota lore, it links the surface world, where humans dwell, with an underground realm peopled by spirits who keep the buffalo and other animals. For ages, those keepers allowed buffalo to issue from the hole in abundance. The creatures emerging from the nether world were quite small and easily passed through the opening, but as their lungs filled with fresh air, they expanded and flourished. And so the Lakota were ensured an ample supply of game—until white men swarmed over the land and troubled the spirits, and the buffalo dwindled to a precious few.

2

THE WAYS OF FAMILY AND CLAN

Two Blackfeet women boil strips of dried buffalo to prepare a meal. Among the Plains Indians, men hunted game while the women did the butchering, cooking, and preserving of meat.

In the late summer of 1680, a small band of Sioux living along the upper Mississippi River in present-day Minnesota invited a French adventurer named Louis Hennepin to join them for a feast of fresh buffalo meat. No sooner had the Indians and their white guest finished eating than a dozen or so angry warriors armed with war clubs burst in upon them. Hennepin watched in shock as the warriors set about demolishing the lodge, ransacking the belongings of his hosts, and confiscating every morsel of leftover food. It suddenly dawned on the startled Frenchman that he had seen the intruders before. This was not an enemy war party but a group of Sioux tribesmen whom he had met at a large encampment only a few days earlier. Afterward, Hennepin learned that they were Dog Soldiers, or tribal police, come to punish their kinsmen for selfishly killing buffalo before the onset of the great communal hunt that was to provide the entire tribe with most of its sustenance for the coming year.

"One of them, who called himself my uncle, told me that those who had given us victuals, had done basely to go and forestall the others in the chase," Hennepin recalled, "and that according to the laws and customs of their country, 'twas lawful for them to plunder them, since they had been the cause that the bulls were all run away, before the nation could get together, which was a great injury to the public."

The scene of retribution Louis Hennepin witnessed was Plains Indian justice at work, for his hosts had violated the most fundamental principle of Plains life—they had put their own welfare above that of the community. The enforcement of an exacting code of behavior was a prerequisite for survival in this unforgiving land, where harsh climate and scarce resources demanded that people live in small, self-reliant, nomadic bands for much of the year. The fate of each individual depended on the actions of the band, and conversely, the well-being of the band rested on the actions of its individual members. Thus, the tribes of the Plains developed communities that encouraged cohesion and harmony and established rules to reduce conflict. Central to those communities was an elaborate system of social bonds and roles. Everyone, from the youngest child to the oldest grandparent, had a place within the group. No one was left out or deemed unessential.

An individual became a recognized member of a Plains community at his or her naming ceremony, usually held soon after birth. Before this ceremony, a baby had no human identity. Infants who were stillborn or died before they could be given a name were neither mourned nor given burial rites, for they were considered to have remained part of the spirit world.

The Mandan believed that the spirits of these nameless children returned to an earth lodge in the hills of the tribal homeland in present-day North Dakota, where an old man cared for them until they could be born again. Childless Mandan women made pilgrimages into these hills to pray for a baby. If a woman wanted a daughter, she brought along a ball and girl's clothing; if she wanted a son, she carried with her a miniature bow and arrow.

Being chosen to name a child was a great honor in every Plains tribe. Parents often asked renowned warriors or men with links to supernatural powers to name their sons, and older women with impeccable morals to name their daughters. Sioux boys were generally named after their oldest living grandparents or, if those names had already been taken by older brothers, after the warlike deeds or accomplishments of their fathers.

A female child usually retained her name throughout her lifetime, although her parents or siblings might hold a renaming ceremony for her if she became sick or suffered some other misfortune. The new name was thought to bring her better luck. A man, however, often received a new name during early adulthood—after he had returned from his first suc-

In an engraving from an 1833 Karl Bodmer painting, Piegans gather at their summer camp outside Fort McKenzie, a major trading post in present-day Montana. Most Plains tribes broke up into small bands during the winter and reunited for celebration and ceremony during the summer.

cessful war expedition, for example, or upon receiving a powerful vision in a dream. The new name was usually chosen from among those of esteemed deceased members of his father's family.

John Lame Deer, a Miniconjou Sioux, has described how he came to take the name of his great-grandfather, who died fighting U.S. Army troops in the late 19th century: "I was asleep, yet wide awake. Then I saw a shape before me. It rose from the darkness and the swirling fog of my earth hole. I saw that this was my great-grandfather, Tahca Ushte, Lame Deer, old man chief of the Miniconjou. I could see the blood dripping from my great-grandfather's chest where a white soldier had shot him. I understood that my great-grandfather wished me to take his name. This made me glad beyond words."

Although the children of distinguished men enjoyed some special treatment—the Blackfeet called them *minipoka,* or "outstanding children"—the concept of inherited status was rare among the Plains peoples. Individuals earned honor and the respect of others as a result of their own actions and character. Talented artisans, such as women with rare quilling or tanning skills, were also highly respected, as were shamans, or medicine men, whose ability to commune with the supernatural powers gave them special insight into the sacred order and structure of things. But this meritocracy was most clearly defined in the choosing of tribal chieftains: Peacetime leaders were selected for their wisdom and good judgment, war chiefs for their courage and prowess in battle.

Wealth on the Plains was measured not by how much one owned, but by how much one gave away. The more generosity a man displayed, the more prestige he attained. The mere possession of many horses

might have elicited envy, but not admiration. To be admired for his horses, a man had to have shown bravery in obtaining them. To have boldly
stolen them from under the nose of the enemy, for example, was especially praiseworthy. The man could then further enhance his prestige by lending the horses to less fortunate tribe members for use in hunting or hauling.

A Sioux male could also gain distinction by
adopting a younger man through a ceremony known as
Hunkayapi, or "Making of Relatives." Forever afterward, the older man
would be obliged to treat the younger as a son, sharing his horses and
other belongings with him, rescuing him from danger during a battle or a
hunt, and caring for him in illness.

According to legend, the ceremony originated with a Sioux medicine
man named Bear Boy, who during his travels once happened upon a
patch of corn. Unaware that the corn belonged to an enemy tribe, the
Arikara, a Caddoan-speaking people closely related to the Pawnee, Bear
Boy dug up the plants and brought them back to his people. To retrieve
their sacred corn, the Arikara sent emissaries to the Sioux bearing gifts of
tobacco. At Bear Boy's urging, the Sioux accepted the offering and made
peace. Bear Boy then created the Hunkayapi rite, which he had received
in a vision, as a means of bestowing the gift of patronage by extending
the Sioux familial ties to non-family members.

A Sioux father could also bring honor to himself and his family by
hosting the Tapawanka Yeyapi, or "Ball Throwing," ceremony for his
daughter upon the announcement of her first menses. At the conclusion
of this celebration, the girl would repeatedly throw a red painted ball into
a crowd of visitors. Each time the ball was caught, its recipient would
receive a horse or other gift from the girl's father. After the father had
given away all of the possessions that he had accumulated for the ceremony, he would invite the guests to join his family in a feast.

The ultimate gift-giving ceremony, however, was the Sioux ritual that
climaxed a year of "spirit keeping" for a child who had died. At the time
of death, the bereaved parents placed a lock of the deceased's hair in a
tiny quilled bag filled with sweet grass. Such a bag, they believed, preserved the youngster's spirit. As they lovingly tended their child's spirit,
the parents collected as many valuables as they could, including horses,
cooking utensils, moccasins, robes, and other articles of clothing. When
they felt they had accumulated enough property to honor their child, usually after about a year's time, the parents held a special feast known as

To protect her child from evil, a Plains mother typically sewed its umbilical cord into a leather pouch. Lizard-shaped pouches such as the one above, commonly used for boys, conveyed the reptile's swiftness and agility. Turtle-shaped sacks, for girls, bestowed that creature's longevity.

Ihta Hepi Wakicaga, or "Through with the Spirit Keeping within a Day." During this ceremony, they released the child's spirit so that it could begin its journey to the land of the dead where it would be born again.

The parents gave away all of the items they had assembled. Those people in the community who had honored the dead child's spirit during the previous year, as well as those who were especially poor and needy, were called forward to choose first from among the gifts. Even the family tipi was dismantled and given away. Then, as a final gesture of generosity and love, the parents disrobed and distributed their clothes among the guests. Without possessions of any kind, the couple was free to begin life anew. But parents who sacrificed in this grand manner did not remain destitute for long. Within a few days, relatives and friends would gather to present them with new clothing, a tipi, and other household essentials.

Because social status among the Plains Indians was neither predetermined by birth nor fixed for life, any individual could aspire to a position of prominence. The oral histories of the tribes abound with stories of unlikely youths who rose to leadership through their exceptional skills or good deeds. One of the most popular of these tales involves an orphan boy who is adopted by a poor old woman. Both the boy and the old woman are too proud to ask for help, choosing instead to pitch their weather-beaten tipi on the outskirts of the main encampment where their poverty will go unnoticed. The boy asks the old woman to make him a bow and arrows so that he can provide her with food in return for her kindness. The weapons she makes take on supernatural power, enabling the boy to kill each animal he hunts with a single shot. Soon he and the old woman enjoy such an abundance of food that even in times of scarcity, they are able to provide meat not only for themselves, but also for the entire community. The boy grows up to become a respected tribal leader.

As this story of the Boy Hero indicates, the Plains Indians, like other Native American peoples, believed that mysterious sacred powers could have a decisive influence on the course of an individual's life. These powers were often unseen, manifesting themselves in the form of dreams and visions. The Indians perceived these dreams and visions to be direct communications from what some tribes called Wakan Tanka, the Great Mystery. Through a dream, a person learned which special talents or abilities—hunting, leadership, medicine making—he or she possessed. These skills helped define the individual's life path. A man who received the power of healing, for example, would aspire to become a shaman.

Sometimes, Plains Indians experienced their powerful, life-shaping

dream during a period of extraordinary stress or grief, or during a serious illness. More frequently, however, the dreams were deliberately solicited during an emotional and physically demanding ordeal known as a vision quest. A man, and in rarer instances a woman, hiked to an isolated location—perhaps a wind-swept bluff or an ancestral grave site. The quester abstained from food and water, hoping to elicit compassion from the supernatural beings. Among some Plains tribes, it was common practice to slice off tiny bits of flesh from an arm to use as an offering, or even to cut off a finger joint in order to arouse the spirits' sympathy. The vision seeker wept continually, pleading with the spirits to show mercy. During the course of a man's vision quest, wives, sisters, and other female relatives sometimes helped attract the attention of the sacred powers by praying at home. In uncommon cases, a wife might fast along with her husband. Such a woman was considered highly spiritual and was much esteemed.

A Cheyenne cradleboard made about 1900 consists of an extravagantly beaded cotton pouch lashed to a wooden frame. With it, a woman could either carry her infant on her back or prop the child comfortably upright against any sturdy support.

Vision quests usually lasted four days and nights, but sometimes ended sooner. The coveted vision might appear while the seeker was awake, or it might come in a dream, after exhaustion and hunger had caused the quester to lose consciousness. The spirits often took the forms of animals or birds. The type of creature that appeared in the vision indicated which gift was being bestowed by the spirits. John Lame Deer experienced a vision in which he joined the "fowl people." He remembered a voice telling him: "You are sacrificing here to be a medicine man. You will learn about herbs and roots, and you will heal people. You will ask them for nothing in return. A man's life is short. Make yours a worthy one."

No animal spirit outranked another. To dream of a large creature, such as a bear or a buffalo, conferred no more status than to dream of a lowly dog or rabbit. Indeed, among the Crow, dreaming of a mosquito meant the person was destined to become a tribal leader.

A spirit might also manifest itself as a rock, a body of water, a crash of thunder, a flash of lightning, or a celestial being—the moon, a planet, or a star. In addition, a spirit could appear as a human or half-human creature, or as a scene or event of which the dreamer was a detached observer. In 1872, at the age of nine, the great Oglala Sioux holy man Black Elk had a vision in which his soul separated from his body and soared into the sky, from where it witnessed a remarkable scene back on earth. "Flames were rising from the water," Black Elk said, "and in the flames a blue man lived. The dust was floating all about him in the air, the grass was short and withered, the trees were wilting, two-legged and four-legged beings lay there thin and panting, and wings too weak to fly."

In his dream, Black Elk saw himself descend to earth where he slew the blue man—a Sioux symbol of drought—by piercing his heart with a spear made of "sharp lightning." Amid loud claps of thunder, Black Elk then rode back into the sky where he met with the six Grandfathers, or Powers of the World, who took him to the "high and lonely center of the earth" to gain a deeper understanding of life. "While I stood there, I saw more than I can tell, and I understood more than I saw," he said, "for I was seeing in a sacred manner the shapes of all things in the spirit, and the shape of all shapes as they must live together like one being. And I saw that the sacred hoop of my people was one of the many hoops that made one circle."

Because his dream contained so many powerful spirits, Black Elk grew up believing he had been bestowed with both warrior and healing powers. The appearance of thunder in his vision led him to adopt a spotted eagle as his personal symbol, for thunder was al-

Fluffy down (right) from the cattail plant (below) was stuffed into diapers to keep babies warm during cold-weather journeys on the Plains. Fresh wads of this natural insulation were added when needed.

ways described by his people as a giant bird. He wore a single eagle feather across his forehead and painted a likeness of an eagle on his war pony. He also made eagle feathers part of his medicine bundle, the personal collection of talismans that was put together by an Indian who had received an important vision. The objects chosen for the bundle symbolize the power given to the individual by the supernatural helper.

Many people had multiple visions during their lifetimes. Others, however, lived their entire lives without experiencing a single significant dream. "Not all who slept on mountains got power," explained a member of the Gros Ventre tribe named The Boy, who died in 1956 in his eighties. "Lots got nothing; they didn't even dream. Only a few got power from such a quest. Some tried over and over again but never got anything. A man might spend five to seven days on the mountains and yet not even dream. If, say, 30 or 40 slept on the mountains, only three or four of them might get power. After a man got to be really old, he no longer tried." Some Plains Indians believed that the spirits sent good luck to such people in appreciation for their repeated efforts to obtain a vision.

Among several tribes, people who did not acquire power through a vision could buy it, or receive it as a gift from someone else. Such purchases could also be made when someone wanted additional power. An inexperienced, younger person or one whose medicine had not worked, for example, could buy an older warrior's bundle or the right to paint himself and his possessions with the pattern of the seller's medicine. The older warrior would teach the younger man the sacred songs associated with his medicine. Women could also purchase power—a decorative pattern that someone else had obtained in a vision, for instance, or the right to practice a specific healing art. Among the Gros Ventre, it was quite common to buy love medicine, although few women purchased it directly from men because the payment might include sexual favors.

Visions bestowing healing powers were considered to be among the greatest spiritual endorsements a person could possess, and they earned the recipient tremendous respect. Seldom, however, could a person who received such a vision embark immediately on a healing career. Usually the supernatural helper would designate to the dreamer the number of years he or she must wait before beginning practice. The waiting period often required an apprenticeship with an established medicine man or woman who would teach the novice the taboos and ceremonies associated with the particular power. Supernatural helpers also imparted such information to the initiate in subsequent visions. A Gros Ventre healer named Little Man told of being shown a special medicinal root by a bear spirit. He did not recognize the root at first, but later, following the instructions of the spirit, he was able to find where it grew on the prairie.

Most healers could use only those powers specified in their visions. A woman might be given the ability to treat colicky babies, or a man the skill to stop a hemorrhage. Little Man was told in a dream that he was being granted the power to help women keep from becoming pregnant, although he was to practice this medicine only on women for whom bearing a child would be physically dangerous. In rare instances, a person was granted overall healing powers. Such a person was considered especially blessed by the spirits.

Some Plains tribes encouraged young children to have visions. Mandan parents often instructed their eight- and nine-year-old youngsters to fast, hoping they would receive visions. Most tribes, however, thought that puberty was the most propitious time for this life-shaping experience. Teenage Cree girls were made to fast and spend four days in seclusion in a small tipi at the onset of their first menstrual period to make them receptive to visions. Most young men and women needed little encouragement to make the quest. They had already witnessed the prestige and success that accrued to those possessing supernatural power.

Beyond their individual visions and achievements, every member of a Plains tribe held a firm place within a great extended family. Parents, children, grandparents, unmarried aunts, and uncles—all lived and camped together. The men hunted together, and when they returned with game to their campsite, the women joined together to prepare the meal and process the hides. The elderly members passed on their experience and knowledge to the young, who in turn accepted the responsibility of looking after their aged relatives when they grew too old to take care of themselves. These large, extended families were part of even larger clans, the groups of related families that served as the basic units of social organization on the Plains. Some tribes, such as the

Blackfeet Indians burn foot-long braids of sweet grass (Anthoxanthum odoratum) to create a sacred, purifying incense for daily prayer sessions as well as special ceremonies. The perennial grass grows throughout Canada and the northern United States.

Before embarking on a vision quest in 1973, a Sioux named Leonard Crow Dog burns sweet grass before a buffalo skull, thereby cleansing himself with the plant's pungent smoke and soliciting the help of an animal cherished by Plains peoples.

Sioux, had loosely affiliated patrilineal clans; when a woman married, she joined her husband's clan, and all of their children became associated with that clan as well. Among other tribes, such as the Crow, clan membership was matrilineal and more exclusive, although it did not prevent the families of both parents from playing active roles in their children's lives.

Many Plains clans had colorful or humorous nicknames. The Crow clans, for example, included the Filth Eaters, the Bad War Deeds, and the Greasy Inside the Mouths, while the Sioux had clans named Wears a Dogskin Round the Neck, Breakers of the Law, and Not Encumbered with Much Baggage. The Crow credit their legendary hero, Old Man Coyote, with doling out some of their most unflattering names. He was said to have given the Uuwuutasshe, or "Greasy Inside the Mouths," clan its name because the original members always ate the fatty portions of their meat.

Other clans and their ancillary groups took their names from physical traits. One Cheyenne family, for example, was called Narrow Nose Bridge because its members had narrowly set eyes. Still other clans bore the names of an animal or a natural phenomenon. The Mandan had the Prairie Chicken, the Speckled Eagle, and the Badger clans, while the Omaha were represented by the Elk, the Wind, and the Deer families. Another Omaha subgroup was called the Do Not Eat Buffalo Tongues because of the taboo imposed on that part of the animal.

The Crow use the phrase *ashmmaleaxia,* meaning "as driftwood lodges," to describe the clan concept. Just as pieces of driftwood naturally come together in the turbulent waters of a river or stream, they reason, so individuals must join together in family clans to successfully traverse life's perilous journey. The metaphor is meant to describe a spiritual rather than a physical journey, for all the family units of a particular clan seldom actually lived or traveled together. Most clans were too large for such an arrange-

This ornate shield bearing two herbal medicine bags and trimmed with eagle feathers belonged to an eminent Gros Ventre warrior named Bull Lodge, who created it about 1860 after it appeared to him in a dream. The concentric circles at its center symbolize the Plains Indians' belief that all things in the universe are interconnected in a divine and harmonious fashion.

ment to be practical. Furthermore, strict taboos about marrying within one's own clan made it preferable to intermingle with the families of other clans. Yet even if they did not personally know all the members of their clan, Plains Indians took their affiliations seriously. They knew that membership demanded special obligations, such as protecting fellow clansmen in battle and even bearing the moral responsibility for the misdeeds or crimes of fellow members.

The importance of the extended family in Plains life is reflected in the complex terms family members use to describe their relationships. Each tribe had its own unique systems of denoting kinship. Thomas LeForge, who was adopted by the Crow in the 1860s at the age of 18, claimed that trying to understand how Crow families referred to one another was one of the most confusing aspects of his new society. Of course, to the Crow, their kinship terminology makes perfect sense.

Most Plains Indian languages have separate words for older and younger brothers and sisters. Among the Crow, females use a different word for father than males do. Other distinctions, however, are not made. Within their clan group, Crow children, like most Plains children, call their uncles "father" and their aunts "mother." By natural extension, the children of all these "mothers" and "fathers" are considered siblings.

These kinship terms indicate the integrated nature of a traditional Plains family. The children always had many people to look after them. An aunt or grandmother, rather than a mother, might take responsibility for teaching a girl beadwork and quilling or the art of dressing animal skins. A boy might go on his first hunting trip under the watchful eye of his grandfather rather than his father, and when he returned to camp with his first deer, an uncle might honor his achievement by singing a celebratory song. In addition, older children shared with adults the responsibility of disciplining their younger brothers and sisters, although such discipline was seldom harsh. Plains children were rarely spanked. Misbehaving youngsters were more likely to have water splashed on them or to be told that a bogeyman in the shape of a coyote or an owl would get them if they continued their naughty ways.

Parents used love and reason rather than punishment to instill ethics and etiquette. "We never struck our children, for we loved them," a Sioux woman said. "Rather we talked to them, gently, but never harshly. If they were doing something wrong, we asked them to stop."

Relations between Plains children were also exceptionally warm. George Grinnell, a scholar who lived among the Cheyenne in the 1890s,

marveled at how infrequently the Indian children grew angry with each other or showed jealousy or resentment. "Two boys might be seen swaying to and fro in a wrestling bout," he wrote, "each encouraged by the shouts of his partisans among the onlookers, and each doing his best. When finally one was thrown, all the spectators raised a great shout of laughter, but he who had been overcome arose laughing too, for he realized that the others were not ridiculing him, but were showing their enjoyment of the contest they had witnessed. The importance of living on good terms with their fellows having been drilled into them from earliest childhood, they accepted defeat and success with equal cheerfulness."

Brothers and sisters enjoyed especially strong bonds of kinship. As young children, they frequently played "village" together, an elaborate, long-running make-believe game in which they mimicked the daily activities of their elders, from setting up camp to hunting buffalo. When they grew older, brothers served as the protectors of their sisters, and sisters spent long hours making robes and moccasins for their brothers. But after childhood, their close, day-to-day interaction ended. Grown-up brothers and sisters were no longer permitted to look directly at each other and had to speak to each other through intermediaries. If a brother walked

Cheyenne girls play with dolls and tiny tipis in this photograph that was taken about 1900. To prepare her daughter for the woman's task of constructing, assembling, and maintaining a real tipi, a mother used a succession of models that were nearly identical to the real thing except in size.

into a tipi and found his sister alone, he would have to turn around and leave immediately. To do otherwise would be to show disrespect.

Most Plains tribes also practiced an avoidance taboo between sons-in-law and mothers-in-law, both of whom were forbidden to look at or speak directly to each other. In some tribes, the taboo was so strict that a man had to avoid uttering any word that was part of his mother-in-law's name. These customs served as a reinforcement of the rule banning marriages between siblings and other close relatives. Yet the relationships remained close throughout their lifetimes, especially between a brother and a sister. A Mandan brother, for example, usually brought his sister fresh meat from his hunting expeditions, and when returning from a raiding expedition, he would present her with the best mare he had captured. For her part, she helped him obtain any items he might need to enhance his status within the tribe. And if he was killed in combat with the enemy, his sister would lead the mourning ceremony for him.

Sisters sometimes even followed their brothers into battle. A Cheyenne elder named Buffalo Hump told George Grinnell of a girl who saved her brother's life after his horse was shot out from under him. The sister fought by her brother's side until another warrior could bring up a fresh horse to rescue them both. A Cheyenne girl named Buffalo Calf Road Woman

Sioux grandmothers traditionally created dolls like the female (left) and male (right) ones shown above in order to teach their grandchildren about the appropriate dress, conduct, and work of women and men.

made a similar defense of her brother and was honored by having the battle in which she fought named Where the Girl Saved Her Brother.

In stark contrast to the respect and formality that characterized relations between brothers and sisters, Plains Indian cousins and, in some tribes, brothers- and sisters-in-law treated each other with excessive familiarity. These joking relatives, or *iwatkusua,* as they were called by the Crow, openly mocked and teased each other, often to the point of public humiliation. A man might be berated by a relative for always wearing old clothes or for failing to bring back a horse or other bounty from a raid. A woman might be ridiculed for being lazy, unattractive, or promiscuous. Although such comments would be considered highly impertinent and rude when coming from an outsider, they were tolerated and even indulged when the source was a jesting relative. The recipient was not allowed to get angry; to show resentment or displeasure only brought on more humiliation and derision.

Iwatkusua also played practical jokes on each other, from such seemingly harmless pranks as reversing the smaller front wheels of a relative's wagon with the larger rear wheels, to the more extreme offense of cutting off the other person's hair. The latter action was considered so severe, however, that the practical joker frequently was required to follow it up with the gift of a horse or other valuable possession.

The joking relationship served practical purposes within Plains societies. It created an accepted process for publicly chastising or censuring someone who had broken the tribe's social norms or otherwise acted improperly. Who better to shame a person for his or her offensive actions than a family member? Among brothers- and sisters-in-law, the joking relationship also helped ease sexual tensions that might otherwise lead to imprudent intimate relations. At the same time, the familiarity enjoyed between joking in-laws helped ease the way for a marriage between these relatives should such a union become necessary later on—after a warrior lost his life in a hunting accident, for example, or while on the warpath. Plains Indian widows often married their brothers-in-law, who were expected to assume responsibility for their dead brother's family. Similarly, a Plains Indian widower frequently married a sister-in-law.

Although the majority of marriages were monogamous, polygamy was also permitted. Most polygamous marriages involved a man and two or more wives; rarely did a woman keep house for several husbands. Furthermore, a man who desired a plural marriage usually chose his additional wives from among his first wife's sisters. In fact, in many tribes a man who married the eldest daughter in a family had a preemptive claim to her younger sisters once they became old enough to marry. One Hidatsa chief named Small Ankle married a woman named Yellow Head and then subsequently married four of her younger sisters, including an adopted sister with no blood relation to Yellow Head. Sisters-in-law

Blackfeet women play the hand game, a popular Plains diversion. Using deceptive motions, a player passed two differently marked bones between her hands. Her opponent guessed which hand held which object. Men played also, sometimes staking a horse or other prized possession on the outcome of the game.

A favorite pastime among the men of some Plains tribes was throwing a stick through a hoop just inches in diameter (below) as it rolled along the ground. A bull's-eye earned the most points.

made natural choices for additional wives because they were of the same family lineage as the first wife. Thus, no conflict arose as to where the family should live. Nor did Plains women consider it degrading to share their husbands with other wives. A first wife usually welcomed the appearance of a second wife in her home for the daily companionship of another woman and to reduce her work load.

In addition to their families, the nomadic people of the Plains felt a strong affiliation to their hunting communities, or bands, with whom they lived for most of the year. Consisting of several clans, or sizable segments of clans, a band was large enough to provide protection against enemy tribes yet small enough to ensure adequate food supplies during the harsh prairie winters. Members of a band pooled their food and other resources and accepted collective responsibility for one another's safety. They had no formal chiefs, but rather agreed-upon leaders, usually experienced older men known for their wisdom, generosity, and skill at mediating disputes. The various bands that composed the tribe came together only during a few weeks in the summer, when they gathered at some predetermined site to visit, trade goods, hold council meetings, and conduct important communal religious ceremonies.

Plains Indians saw their band as a united political and economic entity, but they felt free to merge with or switch to another band should the necessity arise. Occasionally a few families or individuals might leave the band to visit other bands. Sometimes they elected to remain with the new band permanently. A new band might form after an influential warrior left camp, taking sympathetic followers with him. A Cheyenne band once banished a warrior named Buffalo Chief after he killed two fellow members while acting as head of the Dog Soldiers, or camp police. Buffalo Chief then gathered up friends and relatives and struck out on his own.

Like individual clans, each band had its own nickname. Some bands were named for a personal characteristic of one of their past or present leaders, such as the Cheyenne Scabby Hand band, named after an early leader who had a skin disease, and the White Wolf band, named after its founder, a man who was said to have been as crafty and ill tempered as a wolf. Other bands took their names from the areas where they camped, such as the Opposite Assiniboin band of the Gros Ventre who assembled each year along the upper Missouri on the eastern border of Gros Ventre territory near the Assiniboin. Unlike clan names, however, which could be traced back for generations and sometimes to the oldest legends of the tribe, band designations changed often, reflecting the constantly shifting structure and character of the Plains Indian hunting communities.

Because they acted autonomously for much of the year, individual bands had the potential for wielding considerable political power within the larger tribal organization. In a few rare instances, one or more bands split from the rest of their tribe to permanently seek their own fortunes. Rivalry among bands from the same tribe was usually neutralized, however, by the existence of a great web of social clubs, or societies, that cut across both family and band lines. The types and functions of these societies varied widely, from the Sioux Elk Dreamers, whose members used the powers they had acquired to conduct ceremonies concerning matters of love and sexuality, to the Crow Tobacco Societies that were devoted to performing rituals related to the growing and harvesting of the sacred tobacco plant. Membership in a so

Black Plume, a Blood Indian, stands before his tipi with his two wives and favorite horse in this 1892 photograph. Among Plains Indians, monogamous marriages were typical, but a prosperous man might take additional wives to help with the festivities his status required him to sponsor.

ciety conferred considerable social status; the top-ranking societies in each tribe accepted only people of proven reputation.

Although membership in some societies was open to both sexes, most of these groups were either exclusively male or exclusively female. The male societies centered on hunting and warfare, the female ones on farming and crafts. Arapaho women, for example, could join a guildlike society for quillworkers, who practiced the arduous craft of embroidering dyed porcupine quills on clothing, shoes, cradles, and other objects. Members of this prestigious group met in a selected tipi from which men were excluded. Each woman received a medicine bag containing incense, paint, and special tools for marking and sewing. When a member wished to begin a major quilling project—a ceremonial robe or a cradle cover, for example—she called a meeting of the society. A feast would be held, followed by a ceremony in which the older members related stories of past robes they had ornamented. As part of the ritual, the women would give a horse to a poor person in their community.

The Cheyenne had a similar all-female society for tipi decorators. "The first decorated tipi I made was after I had had my fourth child," one Cheyenne woman said in 1932. "Of course, when I was a girl my mother permitted me to look on when she made decorated tipis. There is a rather long ceremony in connection with the making of tipis. I was very carefully instructed never to disclose the ceremony in the presence of men."

Secrecy was also deemed essential to other women's societies, including the Mandan Goose Society, whose members performed special ceremonies to encourage the corn to grow and to pray for the annual return of the migrating water birds in the spring and fall. The Kiowa had a society known as Old Women. Warriors sought their private counsel and invocations both before and after a raid on an enemy's camp.

The most prevalent and powerful of all the Plains societies were those reserved for the tribe's warriors. Only men could be full-fledged members, although women sometimes performed auxiliary roles. These societies consisted of active and experienced warriors who served not only as the tribe's soldiers but also as its policemen.

When the Crow, for example, gathered for their annual summer get-together, their main chief appointed one of the tribe's four warrior societies—either the Kit Foxes, the Lumpwoods, the Big Dogs, or the Muddy Hands—as that year's police force. Their duties included supervising buffalo hunts, halting unauthorized raids on enemy camps, calming any small disturbance that might flare up within the Crow camp, and generally keeping the peace. They had the authority to punish offenders. A man caught prematurely attacking a buffalo herd, for example, usually received a severe whipping and had his weapons broken. Thomas LeForge, the white man who lived with the Crow people during the 1860s, recalled being caught by members of a policing group after he and two other young men chased some buffalo into the Crow camp as a prank. The animals tore up several tipis. The police banished LeForge and his friends from the camp for a month. "It was a distressing penalty," LeForge remembered, "but we stayed out. We should have received much worse treatment had we violated the order."

The Blackfeet had a society of seasoned and honored warriors called the Brave Dogs, who watched over their camps and helped keep order. This group traced their role within the community to their founder, Red Blanket, who had experienced a vision in which a dog spirit told him about a band of fierce, loyal dogs. Like the animals in Red Blanket's dream, the Brave Dogs protected the people with unflinching faithfulness.

The societies' rituals and activities frequently imitated those of the animals for which they were named. The night before a Blackfeet band was to move to a new campsite, for example, the Brave Dogs performed a ritual in which they circled the old campsite, beating drums and singing, and then curled up and slept on the ground at the center of the camp, much as dogs make circles around a spot before lying down to sleep. The following day, after the rest of the band had moved on, the Brave Dogs lingered behind, eating whatever food remained. They then followed the other members of the band to the new campsite, arriving long after all the lodges had been pitched and the fires were blazing. Despite the fact that the Brave Dogs did not physically assist with the move, they had performed an essential service. By traveling behind the rest of the band, the society provided rearguard protection against enemy raiders.

Young boys growing up on the Plains idolized their tribe's warrior societies. They memorized each society's rules and accomplishments, copied their regalia, and dreamed of the day when they could join their favorite group. In many tribes, boys could associate with societies established especially for youths. Blackfeet teenagers could join the Pigeon Society, a group composed entirely of boys who had not yet received personal power through a vision but who wished to begin preparing for the duties of a warrior. Part of their training involved playing risky games or pranks—antics that were tolerated by their elders, who believed the high jinks helped prepare young men for the rigors of war.

After acquiring power, usually through the ordeal of a vision quest, Blackfeet youths moved up to the Mosquito Society, which entitled them to accompany seasoned warriors on the warpath. If they proved themselves deft and courageous, the young men could then join the Brave Dogs, the primary fighting and policing society of the tribe.

The most skillful fighters among the Crow aspired to two elite warrior groups—the Kit Foxes, renowned for their cunning and bravery, and the Crazy Dogs, who lived by the motto: "It is bad to live to be old; better to die young, fighting bravely in battle." The highest-ranking society among the Blackfeet, however, was the Bulls, a group of esteemed elders, distinguished for their heroism and impeccable war records.

Among the Arapaho, boys entered one of two youth societies—the Blackbirds and the Wild Rosebushes—and advanced with age and experience through a hierarchy of warrior societies. To graduate through the Arapaho ranks, however, men had to purchase the right to learn the specific dances, songs, and privileges of each successive society. The process started when a group of boys about the age of 12 felt that they were ready to join the Kit Foxes, the lowest-ranking Arapaho male society. Pooling their resources, the boys' parents assembled enough goods to

In a photograph taken about 1890, a Sioux woman on the Rosebud Indian Reservation in South Dakota uses dyed porcupine quills (shown below at one and a half times actual size) to embroider leather that will eventually form the top of a moccasin. The hard, stiff quills were softened with saliva to render them pliable enough for embroidery.

THE CRAFT OF THE QUILLWORKER

For centuries, the Plains Indians skillfully transformed the quills of the lowly porcupine into exquisite ornamentation for everything from tobacco bags to buffalo robes. Various legends describe quillworking as a sacred gift from a godlike hero or heroine, and its practitioners, all of them women, formed societies that kept the intricacies of the art a tightly guarded secret. Despite its divine origins, however, quillworking demanded a prodigious amount of earthly toil.

Porcupines were rare on the southern and central Plains, so simply obtaining quills was a tedious chore. Quillworkers in these regions either traded for the precious bristles or persuaded their men to mount hunting expeditions to the Black Hills, where the spiny rodents were abundant. After a porcupine was killed, an artist plucked its quills—hollow, cream-colored tubes tipped with black—and washed them in soapy water. She then dyed them by soaking them with colorful plants or minerals, and spread them out in the sun to dry.

When she was ready to work the quills into a design, an artist tucked the stiff spines into her mouth to soften them, carefully allowing the sharp tips to protrude from her lips. She pulled them out as she needed them, flattening them as she did so by drawing them between her teeth.

In order to adorn a long, slender object such as a pipestem or leather thong, a quillworker simply wrapped the moist, pliable quills directly around it in overlapping turns. Another technique called for braiding the quills with sinew and then winding this plait around the object. To decorate a robe or other large item, a woman first painted a pattern on the fabric or animal skin and then stitched on the quills with an awl and sinew.

Some groups mastered the most difficult of quillworking techniques, the weaving of quills into a lattice of cotton or sinew threads that had been stretched taut on a loom. The narrow bands created in this fashion were usually sewn onto special outfits such as war shirts or dance costumes.

As glass beads became a popular trade item at the end of the 19th century, Indian women turned to the easier art of beading. Quillworking nearly disappeared from the cultural landscape, but a handful of persistent artists, men and women, have kept it alive, preserving the ancient techniques as well as creating new ones.

Artists fashioned pouches like the one shown below from the bladders of buffalo and used them to store their quills. The iron masonry tool at right was employed to flatten the surface of a quillwork design. Although each quill was crushed as it was used, smoothing the finished product gave it a uniform appearance.

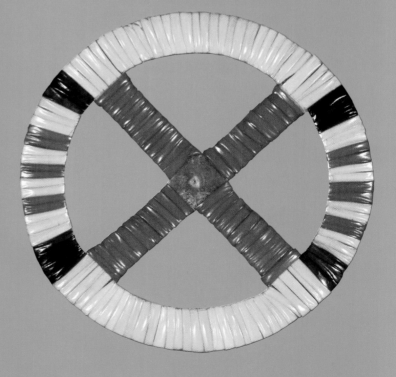

This colorful medicine wheel is made of rawhide wrapped with brightly dyed quills. Plains Indians have used such wheels for centuries to ward off evil and bring good fortune. Quillworkers display some of their finest craftsmanship on spiritual objects.

Sioux artisan Alice New Holy demonstrates one of the quillworking techniques. She began to quill when she was a young girl and, in 1985, received the highest honor the United States can bestow for traditional arts, the National Heritage Master Award of the National Endowment for the Arts.

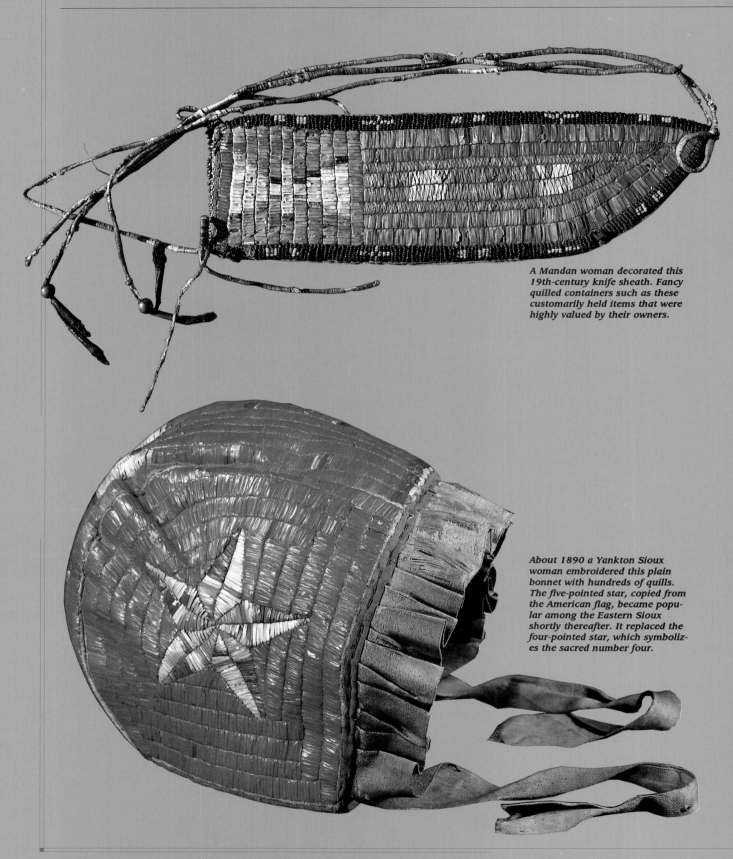

A Mandan woman decorated this 19th-century knife sheath. Fancy quilled containers such as these customarily held items that were highly valued by their owners.

About 1890 a Yankton Sioux woman embroidered this plain bonnet with hundreds of quills. The five-pointed star, copied from the American flag, became popular among the Eastern Sioux shortly thereafter. It replaced the four-pointed star, which symbolizes the sacred number four.

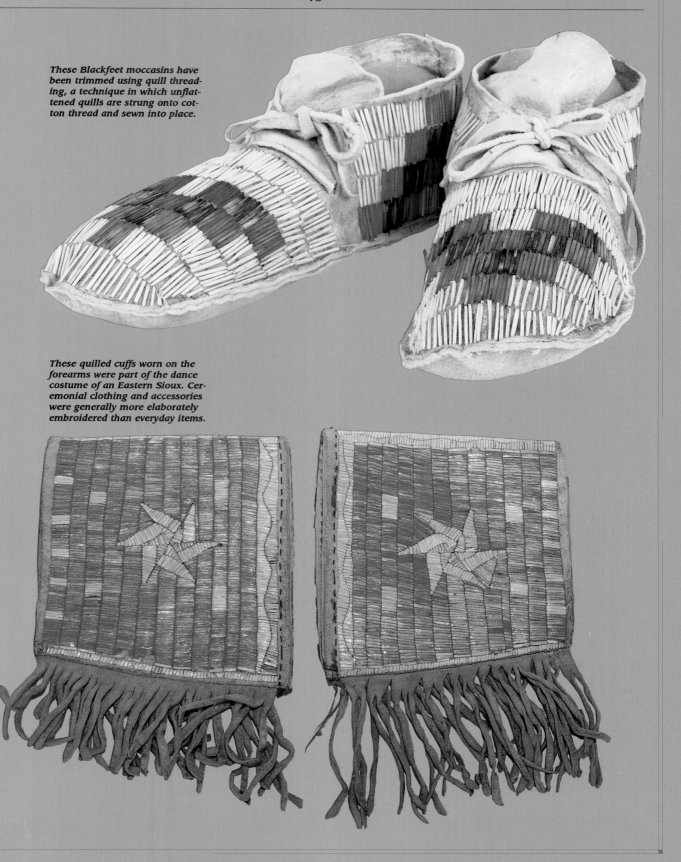

These Blackfeet moccasins have been trimmed using quill threading, a technique in which unflattened quills are strung onto cotton thread and sewn into place.

These quilled cuffs worn on the forearms were part of the dance costume of an Eastern Sioux. Ceremonial clothing and accessories were generally more elaborately embroidered than everyday items.

enable their sons to buy the rituals and insignia of the Kit Fox Society from its current members. To close the deal, the parents sometimes sponsored a lavish four-day feast.

The younger boys did not join the older Kit Foxes, but rather displaced them. The older members then took their newly acquired goods and used them to buy the rights and regalia of the next group, the Stars. And so the rotation continued, up the ranks until it reached the highest society, whose elderly members sold out and retired from the system, dividing their large pile of wealth among them. Every few years, the process repeated itself as yet another set of boys came of age.

In the Crow and Cheyenne tribes, membership in the warrior societies depended not on age level but on similar interests and achievements. Men joined voluntarily, attracted by the organization's reputation and regalia. New members, particularly those who had distinguished themselves in battle, were actively solicited. If a member died, his society usually tried to fill the vacancy by offering gifts to one of his relatives. The more desirable a prospective member, the more gifts were showered upon him. Once they became initiated as members, men rarely switched their affiliation. A notable exception was a Crow warrior named Fireweasel. When Sioux raiders stole all of Fireweasel's horses, his requests for help were ignored by the members of his chosen society, the Kit Foxes. Another society, the Big Dogs, took advantage of this lapse of loyalty and gave Fireweasel new horses and other property. He joined their ranks immediately and remained with them for the rest of his life.

Because there was no hierarchy to soften their rivalries, the warrior societies of some Indian tribes were fiercely competitive. Even though they hunted and raided together on behalf of the entire community, each group looked for every opportunity to publicly flaunt its successes and its rivals' failures. The Lumpwoods and the Kit Foxes, two of the Crow warrior societies of the 19th century, for example, always attempted to be the first to score a coup by touching an enemy with a stick. Whichever group succeeded earned the right to "take away" the other group's songs, which usually meant singing them in a derisive and mocking manner. The losing society could not regain its songs—or its honor—until it touched the enemy first during a subsequent battle.

To entice a lover, a Sioux man might blow softly on an elk-shaped whistle like the one shown below. By imitating the mating call of the elk bull, the man enlisted the potency of that animal in winning a woman's affections.

The drawing above, done by a Northern Cheyenne Indian about 1870, illustrates three couples courting under blankets. A suitor who wanted to speak with his beloved in private met her in front of her family's tipi. Wrapped in his blanket or robe, their heads often hidden from view, the young couple talked quietly and embraced.

Robert Lowie, a scholar who lived among the Crow in the early part of the 20th century, learned from a Crow elder about an incident that had occurred in this age-old rivalry many decades earlier when the buffalo still roamed the Plains. During a skirmish with Crow warriors from both the Lumpwood and the Kit Fox societies, the warriors of an enemy tribe, whose identity is lost to history, found sanctuary on a high butte where the Crow could not get at them. A Kit Fox Society officer, armed only with a coup stick, started up the butte but stopped when he realized that he could go no farther without risking his life. A Lumpwood warrior who had crept up beside the Kit Fox warrior suddenly snatched the coup stick from the hands of his fellow Crow and dashed up the slope. Somehow, the Lumpwood warrior managed to strike one of the enemy warriors with the coup stick. He then plunged the stick into the ground and dashed back to the Crow lines, challenging the Kit Foxes to retrieve their standard. None of them dared go after it. Upon returning to camp, the Lumpwoods asserted their right to take away songs of the humiliated Kit Foxes.

Brash acts such as these were common among the warriors of the Plains tribes. In fact, most warrior societies had clearly defined measures of bravery for their members. To join the Tall Ones, a society that was common to all seven of the Lakota Sioux tribes, a warrior pledged to sacrifice his own life in order to save a wounded comrade. Many Tall Ones died attempting to fulfill that pledge. Before going into battle, the Tall Ones elected four members to the dangerous, yet honored, position of sash bearer. When the sash bearers reached the battlefield, they drove wooden stakes into the ground through the long sashes that they wore around their necks. Thus tethered to the ground, they remained in place until either they were killed or the enemy retreated, in which case a fellow Tall One would come by and pull up the stake.

The societies of other tribes had their own version of the sash bearers. The Mandan Buffalo Bull Society, for example, selected four officers who swore that they would never retreat in battle. Highly admired by their peers, these warriors earned the right to wear special buffalo skull masks during society rituals in order to distinguish them from other members.

Although warriors commanded great respect within all of the Plains communities, the most esteemed members of each tribe were its chiefs, the men and, in rare cases, women who were responsible for keeping peace both within the tribe and with outside nations. In the Crow language, the word for chief is *bacheeitche,* which means "good man." It is an appropriate term, for Crow chiefs, like those of other tribes, were wise and decent men who were selected by their people for their humanity and courage.

The majority of the Plains tribes had a number of chiefs. The Cheyenne, for example, had 44—four principal chiefs and four lesser chiefs from each of the tribe's 10 bands. They held regular councils at which they made the major decisions regarding the welfare of the tribe, such as when to hold a communal buffalo hunt or whether the tribe should go to war.

A sacred Assiniboin clown proudly wears his sect's distinctive regalia. Sacred clowns, common among Plains peoples, donned tattered clothing and grotesque masks during annual ceremonies, and mocked tribal rituals, songs, and sacred objects. By performing what was forbidden, they actually reinforced the notion of good behavior.

Their sacred buffalo horn headdresses resting on stakes, members of the Motokiks Society, a highly secret women's association of the Blood tribe, hold a meeting before their lodge in this early-20th-century photograph. Membership in this elite group was restricted to wives of those men who belonged to the Horns, a prominent male society.

A chief also bore the responsibility of resolving the smaller, day-to-day problems that arose in his particular band. His primary duty was to look out for the welfare of widows and orphans whose husbands and fathers had been killed in battle or in hunting accidents. A chief's second major obligation was to mediate quarrels between arguing members of his band. A chief never took part in any quarrel himself, nor did he ever use his position to enrich himself or his family. Instead, chiefs regularly bestowed gifts on the destitute.

Plains chiefs sometimes showed the same sense of magnanimity to their enemies. The story is told of a Cheyenne leader by the name of High-backed Wolf who once saved the life of a Pawnee man left naked and wounded by Cheyenne warriors. "I am going to help you," the chief told the injured man. "Here are your clothes. Outside are three horses. You may take your choice! Here is a mountain lion skin."

Generosity, honor, loyalty, bravery—ideals that shaped and defined the people of the Plains—were reflected in their choice of leaders. The great Plains Indian chiefs strove for the welfare of their communities with an earnestness and a devotion to duty that has rarely been equaled. Speaking of the Cheyenne chiefs he knew, scholar George Grinnell observed: "True friends, delightful companions, wise counselors, they were men whose attitude toward their fellows we might all emulate." ◈

A DANCE TO THE SUN

At daybreak on the first morning of the ceremony, dancers face the sun to absorb its strengthening power (opposite). They greet the rays with trills blown on eagle bone whistles (below), an action known as "whistling up the sun." The whistles, along with holy tobacco, are the traditional vehicles of prayer in the Sun Dance.

In the winter of 1939-1940, the adopted infant son of a Crow Indian named William Big Day lay desperately ill with double pneumonia in a Billings, Montana, hospital. Ignoring doctors' warnings that the child might die, Big Day took the baby home to the Crow reservation at nearby Pryor. He held him up to the rising sun and made a vow: "If this little boy gets well, I will dance."

The child recovered, obligating Big Day to take part in the most sacred of all Plains rituals, the Sun Dance. Often misperceived by whites as a test of endurance or a rite of passage and once banned by the United States government as barbaric, the Sun Dance stands at the religious core of traditional Plains culture—a great communal prayer in which the participants, after months of preparation, undergo days of physical suffering in order to summon mystic power to aid them in crucial enterprises.

When William Big Day made his vow, the Sun Dance was lost to the Crow, who had not performed it since 1875. To keep his promise, Big Day danced that summer at Fort Washakie, Wyoming, with the Wind River Shoshone, who had recently revived

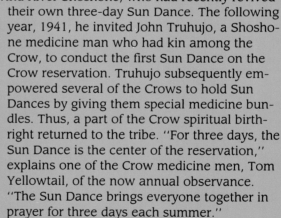

their own three-day Sun Dance. The following year, 1941, he invited John Truhujo, a Shoshone medicine man who had kin among the Crow, to conduct the first Sun Dance on the Crow reservation. Truhujo subsequently empowered several of the Crows to hold Sun Dances by giving them special medicine bundles. Thus, a part of the Crow spiritual birthright returned to the tribe. "For three days, the Sun Dance is the center of the reservation," explains one of the Crow medicine men, Tom Yellowtail, of the now annual observance. "The Sun Dance brings everyone together in prayer for three days each summer."

In 1991 Heywood Big Day—the child who had lain close to death 52 years earlier—celebrated the golden anniversary of the renewal of the Crow Sun Dance by sponsoring the ceremony. Although the Sun Dance is rarely photographed, pictures from that event are shown here and on the following pages.

In a winter rite in which the sun dance medicine bundle is brought out, Samuel Plain Feather sprinkles cedar incense on the coals of a ceremonial fire to cleanse the bodies, minds, and souls of those present, and to send their prayers heavenward with the smoke.

RITES OF PREPARATION

Among the Crow, the Sun Dance was originally an instrument of revenge. A fasting mourner would receive a dream instructing him to enlist spiritual forces against an enemy as prelude to avenging the death of a son or a brother. Today, motives to hold the ceremony include the desire to alleviate the pain of an ailing loved one, to help a relative return safely home from war, to alter one's own personal destiny, or merely to give thanks for current blessings.

As in the past, the dance is usually initiated by an individual, called the pledger, who takes on the entire financial and organizational responsibility for the dance, arranging to build the sun dance lodge, provide the ceremonial feast, and select a knowledgeable priest. In 1991 Heywood Big Day took the unusual step of being not only the pledger but also the priest.

On the site of the 1941 sun dance lodge, and the future location of the new lodge, participants sing sun dance songs to the beat of a drum during a sunset ceremony in April 1991. Heywood Big Day was able to pinpoint the location of the lodge by searching tribal records and by scrutinizing old family photographs.

At the same sunset ceremony, Carson Walks over the Ice (left), a Vietnam veteran, recounts a war deed exemplifying his bravery. The participation of a warrior helps ensure the success of the upcoming dance, an ordeal analogous to war.

A SACRIFICE FROM THE TRIBAL HERD

Traditionally, the buffalo was as central to the Sun Dance as it was to Plains life in general. In Crow society, a dance was preceded by four buffalo hunts led by the pledger. Only tongues and other choice cuts of meat were taken for the ceremonial feast. Acquiring the two large hides to tie the sun dance lodgepoles together required another hunt, for two large buffalo bulls.

Nowadays, the dance is preceded by an abbreviated hunt. Only the pledger, his immediate family, and perhaps a few clan relatives participate, traveling to the Bighorn Mountain pastures to kill one or two buffalo from the tribal herd. Prior to setting out, in accordance with Crow tradition, Heywood Big Day prayed to the Great Spirit for a safe and successful hunt and for permission to kill the buffalo. The hunt started at 4:30 a.m., just before sunrise, and ended shortly thereafter when Big Day's son Bill brought down two animals, each with a single shot.

Spooked by the hunters, bison stream toward a ridge where an old bull stands silhouetted against the sky. Nowadays, the Crow kill buffalo only for ceremonial or other tribally sanctioned purposes.

Big Day and his wife, Mary Lou, remove a slain buffalo's small intestine, considered a good luck charm. As a means of receiving the Great Spirit, the hunting party will eat a sausage prepared from the meat and stuffed in the offal casing.

Standing beside a portion of buffalo meat he has left as an offering to the bears, coyotes, magpies, and eagles, Heywood Big Day says a prayer of thanks. He acknowledges that he has received something sacred and wishes to share it with all of Nature's creatures.

Big Day offers a prayer to the pine tree he wishes to cut down to serve as the "chief pole," the framing member that interlocks with the center pole and serves as one of the lodge's 12 rafters. He promises that the tree will be treated reverently.

BUILDING AND BLESSING THE BIG LODGE

The old Crow term for the Sun Dance is simply the Big Lodge, a reference to the outsize, bare-pole tipi framework—approximately three times the diameter of an ordinary tipi—in which the rites are held. The sun dance lodge is built around a towering center pole—a forked cottonwood trunk, chosen by the pledger early in the winter, cut down, and ceremonially hauled to the site on the day of the dance.

The pole is the symbolic as well as the structural center of the ceremony, representative of the cosmic link between the terrestrial and the celestial worlds. The prayer of one Crow medicine man is an expression of this concept: "Through you we will send our prayers and from you we will receive the blessings from above. Help us."

On the morning of the Sun Dance, the center pole is raised into position with prayer flags and pouches of holy tobacco dangling from its forked branches. The blue banner represents a cloudless sky, night, water, and the heavens; the white banner symbolizes the day, the earth, and purity.

When the pine branch framework of the lodge is complete, a buffalo head, its nostrils stuffed with sage, is attached to the west side of the center pole; a stuffed eagle is hung on the east side. The dancers will fix their gaze on one of the two effigies, or on another focal point on the pole.

LONGING FOR A VISION

The Sun Dance begins at dusk on the day that the lodge is constructed. Back when the ritual was one of vengeance, young Crow men hung from the lodgepoles on thongs attached to skewers run through their chests or backs, and mourners cut joints from their fingers to deposit as offerings. The physical suffering was both a sacrifice and a means of receiving a spiritual vision.

The Sun Dance adopted by the modern Crow, in accordance with the instructions of their medicine fathers, is a less bloody ritual. To obtain a vision, a participant dances continuously, without food and water, until he falls to the ground unconscious. It is in this state that he receives a vision. In the meantime, the dance continues around him. When he regains consciousness, he rises to resume dancing.

Although dancers are allowed to take breaks, those who are sincere in their desire for a vision remain on their feet until their back-and-forth movements wear a groove into the ground. "These dancers are connected to the center pole by an invisible cord coming from the tree and penetrating into their hearts," explains Crow medicine man Tom Yellowtail. "The path that the dancer makes to the center pole represents this attachment. You can see these trails as reminders of the invisible attachment that we all possess to the spiritual domains which are both inside us and yet also beyond us."

On the third and final day, the dancers are given water to break their fast and release them from their vow. They then retire to rest and shower or bathe in the sweat lodge before returning for the feast that concludes the ceremony.

At sunrise on the last day of the three-day ceremony, the exhausted dancers pray to the sun, known to the Crow as the Old Man Above.

Attired in the vibrant robes worn on the second day of the dance to honor the spiritual presence now in the lodge, Heywood Big Day, Jr., rubs himself with purifying cedar smoke. As an expression of humility on the first day of the ritual, the dancers wear simple skirts and dresses.

The dancers carry a small eagle plume and hold an eagle bone whistle between their teeth. With each exhaled breath, the instrument produces a thin, high-pitched noise. The prayers of the participants pass through the eagle bone to the Great Spirit.

3

A BOUNTY FROM THE WILD BEAST

A majestic buffalo bull stands silhouetted against the South Dakota sky. To the Plains Indians, the buffalo was a gift from the Great Spirit that provided both material and spiritual essentials for living. The buffalo hide shield (inset), decorated to represent a Crow warrior's vision of a bull defying its enemies, evokes the spiritual power of the beast.

The lay of the land could not have been better. Eons of gentle uplift and gradual erosion had carved a small cliff in the rolling foothills of the Rockies, near the Sun River in present-day Montana. The drop from the rim was not great, only 30 feet or so, but a clutter of rocky debris at the base of the cliff waited to snag any creature that tumbled over the edge. Back from the rim stretched a verdant pasture much favored by roaming bands of buffalo. The prevailing breezes blew across that grassy plateau toward the cliff, so that the scent of approaching hunters would repel the browsing animals and send them bolting toward the rim. All in all, it was a perfect trap. Native Americans had been using this buffalo jump, as it was called, for at least 2,000 years. Long before horses and guns spread across the Plains, people hunted here on foot, carrying weapons tipped with sharp stone.

When winter loomed and tribes needed to lay by stores of meat and hide for the hard months ahead, scores of Indians trekked to this site to join in the kill. While some members of the hunting party waited at the bottom of the cliff, with bows, lances, and butchering tools at the ready, others crouched patiently in the grass on the plateau above, draped in buffalo robes, until a band of bison drifted between them and the rim. Then the hunters arose, slowly spread out, and began walking downwind toward their quarry. Notoriously poor of sight, the animals scented the danger before they could see it. First to react was the leader of the buffalo band, an alert older cow that snorted in alarm and loped away from the hunters, prompting the other animals to follow. Now the men gave chase, whooping and yelling and waving their robes. Nearing the rim, the panicky beasts pressed together between piles of stones arranged by the hunters to funnel the buffalo to their doom. As the corridor narrowed, the animals in the rear drove the front runners inexorably onward.

There was no stopping at the rim. The old cow vaulted into space, and after her poured an avalanche of twisting, bellowing brown bodies. Many buffalo died outright as they pitched down the rock-strewn slope;

others were maimed, with shattered backs, necks, and ribs; some landed front legs first and somersaulted forward to lie twitching and helpless with broken, dislocated bones. In the settling dust, men with bows and lances moved in to dispatch the wounded animals, followed by women with knives and axes, raising shrill cries of success.

Now began the butchering and feasting, the taking of hides and preserving of meat, and the sundry other rituals of renewal by which the Indians transformed the battered hulks of their prey into the essentials of life. The buffalo in its parts provided virtually all the requirements of human existence, from food and fuel to robes and tipi covers, implements and playthings, war clubs and knives, medicines and sacred objects—more than 100 items in all. For the Plains Indians who drew such bounty from the buffalo, this supremely useful animal was a blessing to be celebrated, and hunters thanked the animal's spirit for offering up its flesh and bone. One early explorer in the Canadian West observed Assiniboin hunters driving a group of prime buffalo bulls into a corral. Preparatory to the slaughter of the animals, the leader of the hunt lighted a ceremonial pipe and symbolically offered it to an old bull within the enclosure. "My grandfather," said the chief respectfully, "we are glad to see you and happy to find that you are not come in a shameful manner, for you have brought plenty of your young men with you. Be not angry at us, though we are obliged to destroy you to make ourselves live."

The generosity of the buffalo to the people of the Plains was unbounded. At the one jump near the Sun River, hunters claimed several thousand animals in the course of a year—so many that those who frequented the site may have accumulated a surplus of preserved meat and other products to offer neighboring groups in trade. Elsewhere, Indians on foot stalked the buffalo in all seasons and with various stratagems—by falling upon the animals as they struggled through snowbanks or across the winter's ice, or by stampeding them into bogs, box canyons, and man-made pens. Abundant evidence of the hunters' success greeted the first Eu-

This six-inch-high wooden buffalo effigy, missing its horns and tail, was carved by a Crow Indian for use in a medicine bundle—a collection of spiritually charged articles whose images had appeared to the bundle owner in a dream or vision.

A medicine sign to attract buffalo, erected by the Assiniboin on the grasslands near Fort Union along the border of present-day Montana and North Dakota, consists of a buffalo skull placed atop an arrangement of boulders and weighted down by a stone. The Swiss artist and explorer Karl Bodmer painted the shrinelike scene in 1833.

ropeans to visit the Plains. Exploring in the Texas Panhandle during the 16th century, the Spaniard Pedro de Castañeda encountered a heap of buffalo bones measuring "a cross-bow shot long, twice a man's height in places, and some 18 feet or more wide."

Beginning in the 1700s, the adoption of horses and firearms made the buffalo hunters of the Plains all the more proficient in their hunting techniques. By the 1800s, the 400,000 or so Plains Indians were killing perhaps as many as two million of these hardy and prolific animals each year. Nevertheless, the Indians still honored their prey and wasted little of what they culled, and the herds remained abundant. Not until whites began to promote the indiscriminate slaughter of buffalo for their hides alone would the long and fruitful relationship that had existed between the Plains dwellers and their cherished quarry be threatened.

The modern buffalo was a formidable creature by any reckoning. A mature, eight-year-old bull might weigh as much as 2,000 pounds, stand six feet high at the shoulder, and measure 10 feet from its snout to the root of its short, tasseled tail. No less impressive than the bull's girth was its great, dark brown cape of luxuriantly curly hair. The cows had somewhat thinner coats and considerably less bulk, with horns that were smaller and more crooked and a mere suggestion of the bull's massive hump.

The females matured around the age of three and bore their first calves in April and early May at the commencement of the bison's—or buffalo's—year. Even so scrupulous an observer as the artist George Catlin gave in and called the animals *buffalo,* although he well knew the difference and wryly commented that they bore about as much resemblance to the Asiatic water buffalo "as they do to a zebra or to a common ox." Yet Catlin was quick to dispel another popular notion—that buffalo always congregated in dense, cohesive herds of many thousands. Actually, for much of the year Catlin found them "dispersed and grazing quietly in little families and flocks, and equally stocking the whole country."

Those "families and flocks" consisted of two distinct aggregations—so-called nursery bands made up of cows and their young, and bull groups made up of mature males. The nursery bands contained anywhere from a few dozen to several hundred animals, including cows, calves, yearlings, and two-year-olds, all of them led by an experienced matriarch. Although many such bands might dot the Plains within sight of a single observer, each assembly kept to itself. The bull groups, for their part, congregated in clusters of a few to as many as 30 animals. Sometimes, when the buffalo bands were widely scattered, careful travelers might pass between them without causing alarm. But the animals were easily agitated, and the bark of a prairie dog, a wind-borne dust devil, or even the shadow of a passing cloud could send every band in the area stampeding wildly off. At such times, the running buffalo tended to coalesce into a churning mass, with the quicker females in the lead, the young males at their heels, the older bulls behind, and the calves frantically trying to keep up. Only after several miles would the exhausted animals slow to a halt and start sorting themselves out.

The buffalo in the bull and cow-calf bands came together by the thousands in July and August during the rutting season. This great convergence of animals was the occasion for bulls that were competing for access to the cows to engage in plunging, head-butting exhibitions. These bruising contests between rival suitors usually concluded when the weaker of the two contestants yielded to pain or exhaustion and broke away, conceding defeat. Sometimes, however, the duel ended in death. A swift slash of horns deep into an unprotected flank, a burst of blood and viscera, and the gored bull would sway and topple over, leaving the winner free to tend to its chosen mate. During the rut, the whole assembly might grow fretful and restless. As Catlin observed: "It is no uncommon thing at these gatherings to see several thousands in a mass, eddying and wheeling about under a cloud of dust; and all bellowing (or 'roaring') in deep and hollow sounds; which, mingled all together, appear, at the distance of a mile or two, like the sound of distant thunder."

Peace returned with the coming of fall. The victorious bulls might remain placidly with the cows and calves for a time, grazing contentedly and enjoying a pleasurable wallow in the prairie mudholes. But as winter approached, the separate bull and nursery bands would re-form and disperse widely in search of browse and shelter from the sharp wind and bitter cold. The buffalo were now in peak condition, sleekly fat after a summer of grazing. The year's calves, yellow-haired at birth and weighing between 25 and 40 pounds, had grown astonishingly—the strongest among them topped 400 pounds. And with the exception of those few individual animals that kept their yellow tint through life and the even rarer albinos, all the recent arrivals had by now acquired the dark brown color of the adult buffalo. If they survived the first perilous winter, these "little black-haired ones," as the Assiniboin called them, would emerge as "blunt horns." In another year's time, they would be "curved horns," and if they attained maturity, some might live to the ripe age of 25. But the odds were increasingly against that as the human occupants of the Plains evolved more and more effective ways of stalking the species.

Considering the enormous numbers of buffalo, it might seem that the Plains Indians would never be out of touch with their prey, that they could follow along the fringes of the herds, taking what they needed whenever they chose. Yet the land was immense beyond imagining, the buffalo fleet and wide ranging, the early Indians relatively few and afoot. Before the advent of the horse, many Plains dwellers were horticulturists who lived in permanent lodges rather than tipis and remained close to their fields and villages for much if not all of the year. They looked to buffalo as an additional source of food and materials, but given their limited mobility, the villagers had to pray that the animals would come their way. Even the nomadic peoples who ranged widely on foot in pursuit of buffalo sometimes faced periods of scarcity, when the animals eluded their traps. When that happened, starvation stalked the tribes, and Indians begged the spirits to bring the buffalo near.

Wearing headdresses made from rare albino buffalo hide, members of the Mandan White Buffalo Society perform a calling ceremony to entice the buffalo close to their village. The women performed the dance during the wintertime when bad weather made long-range hunting expeditions hazardous.

At such times, the Blackfeet set great store by what they called *inis-kim,* or "buffalo stones." Found in streambeds, these were small, exceedingly rare, reddish brown stones that Nature had shaped in the rough form of a buffalo. When the animals were scarce, the owner of such a stone would invite the clan's foremost hunters into his lodge and conduct rites designed to lure the buffalo within range. Other objects, including consecrated buffalo skulls and the round hairballs that the animals sometimes regurgitated, were thought to have a similar power.

Various tribes practiced intricate buffalo-calling ceremonies. Among the most elaborate of these rites were those staged by the Mandan in their villages along the upper Missouri River. As many as 15 men at a time would play the part of the buffalo by donning the animal's pelt, complete with scalp and horns, and dancing in a ring to the accompaniment of songs, rattles, and drums, while hunters carrying bows circled in pursuit. When one of the buffalo dancers grew fatigued, he would slump forward, and a pursuing hunter would target him with a blunt arrow; onlookers would then drag the symbolic victim from the circle and mimic the act of butchering him with their knives, while another dancer took his place. The ritual was intended to honor the noble sacrifice made by the buffalo dancers—and the animals they represented—and so appease the spirits of the buffalo, which would shun the tribe if they felt slighted.

For the most part, the buffalo seemed responsive to such appeals, appearing so frequently that most Plains Indians could afford to be selective in their hunting. The cows and their young were targeted more often than the bull groups—in part because the nursery bands tended to be larger and thus offered greater yields for the entrapment methods of hunters on foot, but also because the hide of the bulls was thicker and harder to work and their meat generally tougher and less palatable than that of the cows and calves. In addition, there were preferred times of the year for hunting. The warm summer months, when the animals' hair was short, were good for taking hides that would be scraped and tanned to produce tipi covers, clothing, moccasins, and other articles. But late fall, before the heaviest snows, was the best time to lure the plump animals into snares and preserve the meat.

Hunting continued on a reduced scale even in the dead of winter, for it was then that the robes taken from the buffalo were at their thickest. Moreover, the Indians loved nothing so much as fresh meat. They looked for buffalo in places where the prevailing wind piled up snow against hillocks, leaving bare spots where the pasturage was exposed—or along riverbanks, where the animals could feed on the bark of shrubs and young trees. One or two men disguised under a buffalo hide often could sneak close enough to a band to shoot arrows at their quarry; alternatively, groups of hunters would slither strenuously through the snow on their bellies single file, like some great snake, until they drew within range of the animals. Whenever possible, the Indians attempted to drive the buffalo into deep snow, where hunters wearing snowshoes were able to approach the floundering beasts and take careful aim with their bows or lances.

Ice was even more advantageous to the Indians. If they could herd a band of buffalo onto a frozen lake, the frantic animals would begin to slip and stumble, becoming easy prey for surefooted hunters. Another productive winter technique was witnessed in the early 1800s by a trader named Charles McKenzie. He reported that Indians along the Missouri would drive buffalo onto the frozen river and "confine them into a narrow space where the ice was weakest, until by their weight and pressure, large squares of ice would give way and vast numbers of the animals were plunged into the water." The current then carried the drowned buffalo under the ice to an opening downstream, "where they again

This Gros Ventre headdress, made from buffalo hide and horns, eagle feathers, and braided horsehair, was worn during the Buffalo Dance, a ceremony designed to lure the buffalo herds to within hunting range.

emerged and were received by crowds of women and children, provided with proper hooks and instruments to haul them onto the ice, which in a short time became strewn with dead carcasses."

When the weather on the Plains turned warmer, one or two hunters might conceal themselves in the tall grass near watering places and target the buffalo as they filed down to drink. In such cases, the outcome depended on the craft and cunning of the individual rather than on the resources of the group. Many hunters carried bows they had made themselves, using buffalo sinew to fashion the bowstring and to reinforce the frame, which was usually carved of strong, limber wood such as juniper or hickory, although some Plains Indians used laminated animal horn instead. The strongest bows could propel an arrow a few hundred yards, but to penetrate the thick hide of a buffalo, the hunter had to position himself within 50 yards or so of his target.

Even for skilled bowmen, stalking buffalo in piecemeal fashion could be time consuming and often frustrating. Whenever possible, hunters preferred to pool their efforts and trap whole bands of animals at a time. For sheer efficiency of slaughter, nothing could surpass the jump-kill technique. Scattered across the northern Plains were more than 40 sites

Seated beside two fellow tribesmen, an Oglala Sioux (left) consecrates a ceremonial pipe in front of a sacred buffalo skull set upon a bed of sage. Buffalo skulls play a vital role in a large number of Plains rituals.

A pair of polished buffalo horns top a ceremonial staff that was made at a time when the great bison herds had been all but eradicated. The staff may have been carried by a tribal leader or used in dances that harked back to the days when buffalo were plentiful.

similar to the bluff near the Sun River—places with such names as Head-Smashed-In, Boneyard Coulee, and Bison Trap—and the Indians exploited them for all they were worth. Another way of achieving the same end was to impound a band of buffalo in a natural cul-de-sac such as a box canyon or in an artificial enclosure, where the animals could then be cordoned off and slaughtered. The Blackfeet were among the first to create their own pens for this purpose, and they called the technique the *piskin*—a "corral" or "pound."

Although simple in conception, the piskin demanded careful planning and precise teamwork by the hunting party, which might include scores of men, women, and children. The corral itself consisted of logs stacked horizontally to a height of several feet and supported by posts planted vertically in the ground, forming an oval that was large enough to hold 100 or more head of bison. Inside, sharpened stakes projected upward at an angle from the base of the wall, reaching to the height of a buffalo's ribs, thus preventing the animals from jamming against the wall and bursting through. At the opening, the Indians often dug a sill that dropped two feet or more to the floor of the pound; the buffalo found it easy to gallop in but hard to escape. To ensure against a breakout, the entrance was sealed off with a sturdy gate once the animals were trapped.

The piskin was often built at the base of a dry gully so that the buffalo would follow a natural pathway down to the opening. As further inducement, obstacles such as cairns or piles of brush were placed at intervals in a long, broad V that spread out for a mile or two onto the prairie. Like the rock piles found at some buffalo jumps, these markers served to funnel the animals toward the enclosure, although members of the hunting party had to stand behind the piles yelling and waving to keep the buffalo from veering off in either direction and eluding the trap.

When a promising band was located, a buffalo-robed decoy, perhaps bleating like a calf, might be sent out to lure the animals into the mouth of the V, while people took up position behind the markers. As the buffalo drifted toward the decoy, hunters moved in behind the animals and prepared to stampede them. One time-honored method of driving the buffalo forward was to set fire to the grass to the rear of the band. Terrified by the smoke and flame, the beasts would charge into the funnel, herded along by the people shouting and gesticulating at the markers. The technique was risky, for the piles of stone or brush were not enough in themselves to contain the animals, and the hunters could be trampled to death if the

Thousands of years before Plains Indians acquired horses, hunters on foot stampeded bison over this precipice—known as Head-Smashed-In—near the Porcupine Hills in Alberta, Canada. Today, layers of bones lie 12 yards deep at the base of the cliff, a testament to countless well-coordinated kills.

stampeding buffalo swerved in one direction or the other. With luck, however, the piskin was soon filled and the gate closed.

Once the animals were impounded, hunters wielding bows and lances stood at the wall and shot or stabbed the animals until all were dead, for it was dangerous for anyone to enter the piskin while the buffalo remained alive. Among the Assiniboin, the slaughter of the animals in one such pen was followed by a brief ceremony. A chief entered the enclosure and paid tribute to the victims by placing a bit of swansdown, colored bright red, on the head of each buffalo. At the conclusion of the ritual, all members of the hunting party were invited to take whatever part of the kill they thought was proper.

These pound drives, as they were called, could yield prodigious quantities of meat. In 1797 a Hudson's Bay Company trader named Peter Fidler was present when a Piegan hunting party took more than 250 buffalo in a succession of pound drives conducted over a six-week period at Stimson Creek in Montana. The Piegan might have killed more, Fidler reported, except that the stench from the butchering operations became unbearable, and they were forced to leave the area. The odor of death could drive away the buffalo as well. Hunters everywhere had to be judicious in their use of the corrals, for it took up to three months for the elements to cleanse the killing ground after a drive.

In most tribes, the task of butchering the buffalo fell to the women, who formed an integral part of the hunting group. They were usually on hand

Comanche horsemen drive bison over a cliff in this 19th-century painting by Alfred Jacob Miller. Such tactics were not for the faint-hearted: The Blackfeet called the places in which they trapped and killed up to 100 buffalo at a time "deep blood kettles."

when the animals were trapped and killed, and they wasted no time in gutting the carcasses with knives and hatchets. Among the Blackfeet, the greatest delicacies—notably the brains, liver, and kidneys—were cut out immediately and eaten raw. Anyone who so chose could quaff a little of the buffalo's blood, or partake of the soft gristle of the nose; older men frequently consumed the testicles of a bull on the spot in the hope that they might make them virile. Then those whose job it was got down to the serious business of skinning and carving up the rewards of the hunt.

Whether bull or cow, the buffalo was a cumbersome beast and no easy thing to handle. The great, thick hide of a fully grown bull weighed as much as 150 pounds, and usually it was taken off in two pieces after the coat was first split down the belly, then along the back. The thinner hide of a mature buffalo cow was regarded as ideal for tipi making, and the Indians took great pains to wrestle with the carcass until they could secure the hide in one piece.

When the hide was off, most parties cut virtually all the edible flesh from the animal, which meant packing several hundred pounds of meat. Once the Plains Indians acquired horses, hunters would sometimes reap such bounty that they could afford to carry off only the tongue and other

Some Plains tribes have traditionally ascribed spiritual power to stones that naturally resemble buffalo. The stones shown here, fossilized shells of a long-extinct mollusk, are part of a Blackfeet medicine bundle.

tender cuts, leaving the rest to the wolves that lingered nearby. But in earlier times, Indians seldom had that luxury. They butchered their catch thoroughly, and if their camp was located some distance away, every able-bodied person helped carry home the harvest. Men, women, and children staggered under heavy burdens, while the camp dogs strained at sledlike travois that supported loads of 60 pounds or more. The dogs were tough and wiry, but a journey of a mile or two might still take them as long as an hour.

Although the Plains Indians supplemented their diet with fruits, tubers, and other edibles whenever possible, buffalo meat was their staff of life, providing most of the nutrients they required. Other creatures—particularly deer, antelope, elk, and fowl such as turkey and quail—were hunted and eaten in smaller quantities by some groups, but many animals were subject to dietary taboos. One bird the Cheyenne never consumed was the magpie, because it was said that in ancient times this colorful relative of the crow had helped the Indians win the contest to see whether the buffalo should eat the people or the people should eat the buffalo. The Blackfeet, for their part, proscribed the eating of bear, wolf, fox, coyote, dog, and even fish—all of which served to increase the reliance of the people on buffalo.

Typically, the Plains Indians consumed two or three meals daily—children and the elderly ate whenever they pleased—and a healthy adult male might devour a pound or two of meat per meal. The basic cookery involved much boiling and roasting. A Plains wife preferred hardwood for her tipi fire: Willow, chokecherry, alder, mountain maple, and cottonwood were best; evergreens were usually too smoky and threw sparks. Considerable imagination went into a wife's cuisine. Greatly admired were a delicate stew made of tender calf and various vegetables, and a hearty, sausagelike dish of meats and kidney suet cooked inside a

The Plains Cree used amulets such as this one during rituals designed to help locate the buffalo herds. The little charm was carved out of wood and wrapped in beaded leather with the features of a buffalo.

The excavation of a geological subsidence, or sinkhole, formed by the erosion of limestone beneath the grasslands outside Sundance, Wyoming, reveals the bones of up to 20,000 buffalo in layers that extend more than 20 feet deep. Between 1500 and 1800, at least five Plains tribes used the site as a buffalo jump, killing the animals by stampeding them over the sinkhole's steep sides.

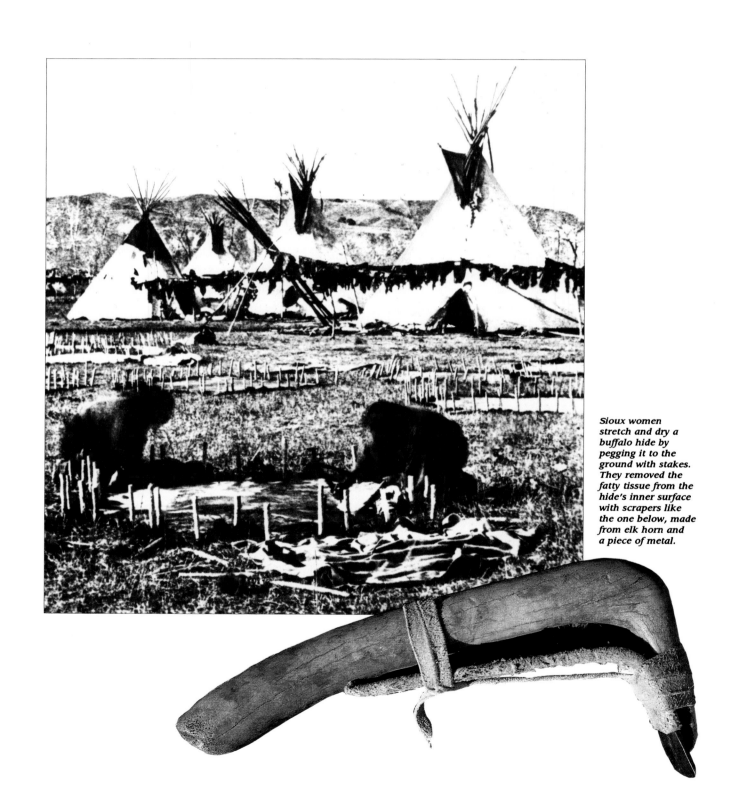

Sioux women stretch and dry a buffalo hide by pegging it to the ground with stakes. They removed the fatty tissue from the hide's inner surface with scrapers like the one below, made from elk horn and a piece of metal.

cleansed intestine. Intestines without stuffing were roasted to a crisp and enjoyed like cracklings, and a sort of buffalo cheese was derived from the milk-filled intestines of newborn calves. Other favorites were a roasted udder filled with its milk and a thick, jellylike pudding of buffalo blood.

For much of the year, the Plains people ate mostly fresh meat, but with the approach of winter, every camp undertook the task of preserving ample amounts for the lean days ahead. The tempo of hunting increased, and women prepared large quantities of long-lasting pemmican by roasting meat and pounding it with a stone maul into a paste that was then mixed with a roughly equal quantity of fat. In addition, strips of meat might be dried in the sun on elevated racks or atop poles to keep them out of the reach of dogs or wolves; it took only a few days for the sun to transform the meat into a jerky that would keep for months. On occasion, the Indians might build fires under the racks to smoke the meat and thus speed the curing process.

A wintering band could survive for weeks on pemmican and buffalo jerky alone. But the preserved rations were less tasty than fresh meat, and Indian families felt deprived when conditions prevented the hunters from making a kill for more than a few days at a time. After a particularly severe winter in the early 1800s, trader Charles McKenzie reported that the Mandan living along the Missouri were so eager for fresh meat that they hauled from the river the half-rotten carcasses of buffalo that had drowned hundreds of miles upstream. "When the skin is raised," he observed, "you will see the flesh of a greenish hue, and ready to become alive at the least exposure to the sun; and is so ripe, so tender, that very little boiling is required—the stench is absolutely intolerable—yet the soup made from it, which is bottle green, is reckoned delicious."

Aside from nourishing the Plains Indians, buffalo furnished them with nearly all their tools and trappings. The animal's horns were carved into cups, or boiled until soft and shaped into spoons and ladles. Its hoofs were turned into glue; its bones into sleds, awls, hoes, and other implements; its hair into braided lariats and pillow stuffing; its sinews into thread for sewing; its stomach, paunch, and heart lining into waterproof containers; its tail into a handy fly switch. Dried buffalo dung not only served nicely as campfire fuel but also could be pounded fine and applied to infants as a soothing baby powder. The tough rawhide of the buffalo was used to make shields, drumheads, moccasin soles, ropes, belts, bags, and coverings for the small rounded vessels known as bullboats. The

Plains Indians used buffalo horn to make eating utensils such as this Sioux spoon, decorated with beads and a carved horse head. Horns were softened in hot water to ease shaping.

tanned hide, meanwhile, was tailored into tipi covers, shirts and leggings, robes, blankets, and diapers.

The true status of a Plains wife in the community depended on her industry and expertise in the working of buffalo hides. So important were these skills that a Cree or Teton girl spent her first menses in four days of seclusion on the outskirts of camp practicing hide tanning, among other useful arts; this would ensure that she grew up to be a virtuous and industrious woman. Hide-scraping tools were prized possessions; men often crafted them as gifts for their brides, and women were sometimes buried with them. Blackfeet women kept track of their accomplishments by means of black and red dots incised on the handles of their elk horn hide scrapers: Each black dot on one side of the handle represented a robe; each red dot on the other side signified 10 hides or one tipi. When a woman had compiled 10 red dots, she could carve a circle on the handle of her tool. A particularly gifted and hardworking woman received an honor mark—a special belt that set her apart from her sisters. She might also offer her services for payment in goods to less-capable women, and thus contribute significantly to her family's wealth.

Depending on the task at hand, a woman might spend as many as 10 days preparing a hide. She first spread the fresh buffalo skin fur side down on a rack and removed bits of fat and flesh. She allowed it to dry in the sun for a day or two, after which she scraped and thinned the fleshy side. If the skin was to be made into something other than a winter robe or blanket, she then immersed it for a few days in a lye solution made from ashes and water; this loosened the hair so that it could be removed easily. Next, she prepared a tanning mixture of buffalo brains and liver, grease, and pulverized soaproot; if an especially white hide was desired, bones were pulverized and the oil extracted and added to the combination, which was then laboriously worked into both sides of the skin. The hide was folded and put aside overnight so that the mixture might penetrate thor-

This buffalo chip, wrapped in a piece of buffalo intestine decorated with colored beads, was part of a Blackfeet medicine bundle associated with the Yellow Buffalo tipi. The chip served as a rest for a sacred pipe during rituals.

These rattles were part of a medicine bundle used by the Blackfeet during Sun Dance ceremonies. They consist of buffalo scrota sewn together with sinew and filled with dried seeds or pebbles.

oughly. The following morning, it was stretched on a rack or pegged to the ground and dried in the sun.

As a final step in the process, the hide maker softened and perhaps thinned the skin by working it over with one of her elk horn tools, taking extreme care not to puncture the leather. Or she might soften it by the use of some other technique, such as pulling it back and forth through a hole in a buffalo shoulder blade, or against a rope braided from buffalo sinew. Many hides were treated further by smoking, which rendered them soft and pliant even after repeated exposure to water.

Preparing the dozen or so hides needed for a tipi was perhaps the plainswoman's most demanding task. But there was a tremendous benefit. The dwelling stitched together from the hides she tanned belonged to her and her alone. If, as sometimes happened, a husband and wife separated, the woman took the tipi with her. Such skill was required to assemble a tipi that the task was supervised by honored lodge makers, who ranked highest among the tribe's craftswomen. After a wife had tanned all the hides and prepared the sinew threads, she asked the lodge maker to cut the sections of her tipi and invited a group of friends to help sew them together, in the manner of a quilting bee. Among the Cheyenne, the lodge maker began by placing a large gob of paint mixed with grease on her head, in the part of her hair; this she would use for marking the skins laid out before her in a rough approximation of the tipi. The lodge maker used no patterns and had only her expert eye to guide her as she marked the skins and then cut them with a sharp knife. When she had finished, the women ate a meal prepared by their hostess and spent the rest of the day sewing and chatting. By nightfall the tipi was ready. The women applied a finish of white clay and water, assembled the lodgepoles, and put up the tipi, stretching it taut and pegging it securely to the ground. The grateful hostess laid out another meal, and then everyone went home.

Soft and pliable, this ocher-powdered Blackfeet storage bag was made from the skin of an unborn buffalo calf. The bag is filled with sweet-smelling fir needles that are burned over a hot coal during particular rituals to purify the participants.

Many tribes hung buffalo hoofs from the wooden pins that fastened tipi door flaps. When the flap was lifted, the hoofs made a rattling noise.

A greater outpouring of effort was required for the large communal tipis that dominated camps and villages throughout the Plains. The council lodge, where tribal leaders convened, might be 30 feet or more in diameter. In addition, warrior societies had their own tipis for meetings and ceremonies, while shamans presided over medicine tipis, painted with spirit designs. Sometimes, upon the death of an important individual, mourners erected a special tipi to serve as a burial lodge; inside, the deceased was placed on a bed or platform in full regalia. But most Plains Indians were laid outdoors on a simple scaffold or in trees after death, facing the sky and the spirits above. In a parting tribute to the animal that gave life to the people, the deceased was often wrapped in a fresh buffalo skin, its fleshy side still moist—a sign of hope and renewal in the midst of decay.

This buffalo tail whisk was wielded in rituals to help heal the sick. It is thought to embody the powerful spirit of the animal itself.

In time, the destiny of the Plains Indians became linked all the more closely to the fortunes of the buffalo through the agency of another animal, introduced by chance on the Great Plains: the horse. With horses as mounts, Indians could pursue the buffalo at will instead of simply waiting for them to wander near traps. With horses as beasts of burden, hunters could carry more meat and hide back to camp before it spoiled, and tribes could more easily shift their campsites in pursuit of their quarry.

This equine revolution, which began around the Spanish colonies of the Southwest in the late 1600s and spread slowly northward and eastward across the vast buffalo ranges, ultimately touched the lives of all Plains Indians. By the early 1800s, almost every family had a few horses, and some could count a remuda of 60 or more. As a result of the greater access to buffalo that horses afforded, Indian populations ex-

Sliding on sleds made from buffalo ribs was a popular winter pastime on the Plains. This Hidatsa model, 15 inches long, with a hide strap for pulling, was used by small children.

panded, trade flourished, and the tribes grew richer. In most places, hunting patterns changed. The Indians still engaged from time to time in communal drives at the old buffalo jumps and piskins. Yet now with a mount that was swifter and more nimble than the buffalo, hunters intent on entrapping their prey relied increasingly on a technique that could be practiced almost anywhere, without resort to natural or man-made snares. Known as the surround, it had been used with some success by hunting parties in earlier times. In its original form, the technique required dozens of Indians on foot to furtively surround a small band of buffalo and move in on them in a rush, yelling and waving blankets. Ideally, this compressed the band into a confused, milling mass that offered easy targets— but it could also result in a stampede, with deadly consequences for the hunters. The danger and uncertainty of the surround were reduced once the hunters operated on horseback. Circling the buffalo band on their mounts, Indians fired flights of arrows at their stunned prey, relying on their horses to elude any buffalo that turned on them.

Even more popular than the surround among hunters on horseback was a freewheeling technique in which the pursuit of the buffalo became a selective, individual endeavor. This was the straightaway chase, executed by a group of hunters who simply rode down the buffalo and killed the ones they chose. Although it demanded less in the way of teamwork, the chase posed an exacting test for both horse and hunter. The buffalo horse, or runner, most often was a four-year-old, an animal at the peak of its speed and stamina that had been chosen from among numerous candidates for a rare combination of qualities: the endurance to sprint for several miles; the intelligence to learn rapidly and respond on command; the surefootedness to race over uneven ground without faltering; the nimbleness to move through a galloping, panic-stricken herd to the chosen target; and above all, the courage to face so huge and menacing an animal as the buffalo without shying. Once an Indian hunter had found

Mounted Hidatsa hunters dash into a roiling mass of buffalo during a surround-style kill. The surround began when two columns of whooping hunters, converging at a gallop, turned the leading buffalo back into the fleeing herd, causing the rest of the terrified animals to run in a circle.

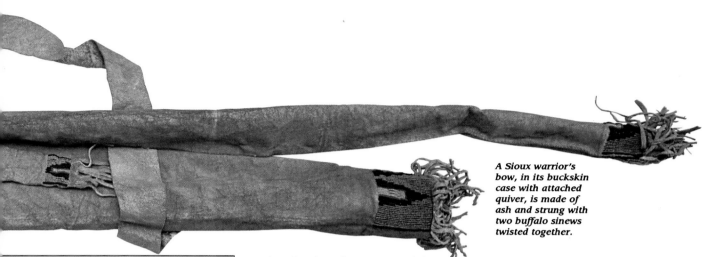

A Sioux warrior's bow, in its buckskin case with attached quiver, is made of ash and strung with two buffalo sinews twisted together.

and trained such an animal, he treated it with loving care; he fed it the finest grasses, bathed it with cool water in summer, and warmed it with buffalo robes in winter. While other horses might be held in corrals at the outskirts of camp, the runner was tethered next to its owner's tipi, where only the boldest of raiders dared venture.

At the time of the chase, when scouts had located the buffalo, the hunter took up his short, powerful bow and filled his quiver with any-where from a dozen to two dozen arrows bearing his personal mark. On his fine horse, he placed a buffalo-robe saddle secured by a wide band of tanned hide; he usually left the cinch somewhat loose, so that he could thrust his knees under the band to brace himself during the run. For a bridle, the hunter used only a thin rawhide thong looped over the horse's lower jaw and tucked into his belt, leaving both hands free to shoot. At the climax of the chase, he guided his runner with his knees and by shift-ing his weight in the direction he wanted to go.

Unlike the hunters using the jump-kill technique, the riders would rarely initiate a chase when the wind was blowing their scent toward the buffalo and warning the animals of the impending danger. If possible, the men on horseback would approach a buffalo herd from the cover of a hill or ravine until they were close enough to charge. Otherwise, they rode slowly up to the buffalo until the lead cow bolted. Then the hunters would race along one or both flanks of the galloping herd, keeping the buffalo together and picking off whatever animals were prime at that time of year. When he had chosen a target, the hunter typically approached to within 10 or 12 paces before loosing his arrow. He knew every bone and organ of his quarry and aimed at a vulnerable spot. One such point lay just behind the last rib about one-third of the way down from the back-bone to the belly. An arrow entering there needed only to penetrate a thin layer of muscle before hitting the intestinal cavity. With luck, it would pierce a vital organ, and the buffalo would drop quickly. Otherwise, the animal might run on for a mile or two before expiring. It often took two or three arrow strikes to down a buffalo.

The wounding of a buffalo brought moments of high peril for horse and rider. The enraged victim often turned and tried to hook its sharp horns into the horse. Mindful of this risk, hunters trained their runners to swerve sharply away at the twang of the bowstring. Yet anything could happen in the dust-clouded melee. A buffalo wounded by one hunter might careen wildly and slam into another man's mount, or a horse might stumble over an unseen rock, a gopher hole, or an old skeleton. An exceptionally swift and nimble Indian afoot might manage to dash and dodge to safety, or a bold man might even leap astride a buffalo, grab its hairy mantle, and ride out of danger. Most often, however, an unhorsed hunter stood little chance in the midst of a churning, trampling herd.

The chase was usually completed in 30 minutes or so, and then the hunters walked their winded horses back through the dead and dying buffalo that lay lumped on the plain. Men finished off the wounded buffalo, searched for their arrows, marked their kills, and pulled out the undamaged shafts. Now was the time for the boys who were too young to participate in the hunt proper to ride out on their ponies and practice their skills on calves that had been left behind. Now came the women with their cutting tools along with the packhorses that each could carry hundreds of pounds of meat. A woman could claim the hides and all the choice cuts from the animals brought down by her man. But she was expected to share the ordinary cuts with the poor, in particular widows with no hunters in their immediate families.

A talented hunter on a superior runner might bring down four or five buffalo in the course of a single chase, and every tribe had its tales of fabulous exploits. The Cheyenne celebrated two remarkable hunters, Big Ribs and Strong Left Hand, each of whom had killed a pair of buffalo with a single arrow, the shaft going clear through the first animal and burying itself in the second. More amazing still was the feat of a Cree bowman, whom tribal tradition credited with slaying 16 buffalo, one after another, while using just 17 arrows. Ordinary hunters were only as good as the horses they rode, but the great ones were like the Hidatsa hero known as The Last Stone—who, in the words of his admirers, could bring down a buffalo "on any kind of horse."

Even a mediocre marksman astride an unexceptional horse might claim two animals during a chase—providing enough meat to feed an extended family of a dozen or more people for a few weeks. And with the horse to carry them wherever they wished, hunters could stay in touch with the herds and cull them liberally for months on end. Over the course of a season, a party of fewer than 20 hunters could bring down 1,000 buffalo. In addition to making tribes more populous and prosperous, this boom in hunting activity, which was stimulated in the early 19th century by a rising demand for buffalo hides among white traders, altered the customs of the Plains Indians. For example, the practice of one man having two or more wives, hitherto restricted largely to chiefs and other prominent figures in the band, became fairly common. It was no trick for an experienced hunter to keep several women busy processing his kills, and since many more men than women died—in the hunt or during the raids and skirmishes that became increasingly common as tribes vied for horses and access to buffalo herds—there were always a number of widows who were looking for husbands.

In most cases, the first wife approved of this arrangement: There was more to do than she could handle, and now as in earlier times, the succeeding wives were often her sisters. All told, a hunter might be responsible for two or three wives and their assorted children by him and by any previous husbands, along with parents, older aunts, and uncles. Thus, there might be as many as 15 people living cooperatively in a cluster of several tipis. Before the advent of the horse, no individual could have hoped to garner enough food, clothing, and material to support so many people. To be sure, providing for such a large family was a source of great pride for a man, but it was also hard work. As one Indian hunter responded when asked if he envisioned continuing his predatory pursuits in the afterlife: "Oh, no! There is no hunting or labor in paradise."

Like the buffalo they stalked, the members of most Plains tribes spent much of the year in bands traveling from place to place in search of sustenance. But those bands often came together in late summer or early fall for a mass encampment, where the tribe as a whole could socialize, dance, hunt, feast, and lay in stores of dried food for the coming winter. During the 19th century, these tribal get-togethers drew as many as 3,000 people, with the hunters among them joining in a series of surrounds and chases on the open plain.

The majesty and excitement of these splendid buffalo hunts stirred the Native Americans to their souls. Black Elk, the great Oglala Sioux medicine man, hunter, and warrior, described how the scouts excitedly

A LANGUAGE OF THE HANDS

As Indian groups evolved on the Plains, they spoke so many different languages and dialects that vocal communication between tribes was difficult if not impossible. In order to express themselves across tribal lines, they developed a remarkably eloquent sign language that most groups came to understand, a system that in a number of tribes endures today.

The Indian pictured on these pages is expressing the idea: "After the white man came here, the buffalo disappeared." The signing is not static, but rather it involves movement of the hands and fingers. Directional arrows and ghosting are employed here in order to show the proper motions.

AFTER . . .

To make the sign for the concept "a long time ago," the hands begin at waist level, angled slightly to the left and with both index fingers extended. The right hand is then drawn back and to the right.

THE WHITE MAN . . .

With the index finger extended and palm facing down, the right hand is drawn across the forehead in order to simulate the brim of a white man's hat.

CAME HERE . . .

While the left hand is held waist high, with palm up and fingers open, the right hand, with the index finger extended, is brought down into the left palm.

THE BUFFALO . . .

The hands are placed on either side of the head with the index fingers slightly hooked, like the horns of a buffalo.

DISAPPEARED . . .

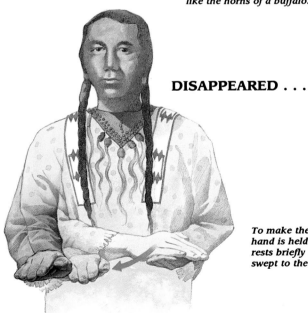

To make the sign for "all gone," the left hand is held out, palm open. The right hand rests briefly on the left palm and is then swept to the right, across the body.

returned with word that they had "seen the good"—an immense herd of buffalo blackening the prairie some distance away. When this news reached the camp, recounted Black Elk, a crier summoned the hunters, chanting: "Your knives shall be sharpened, your arrows shall be sharpened. Make ready; make haste; your horses make ready! We shall go forth with arrows. Plenty of meat we shall make!"

Black Elk remembered how the cavalcade went out to greet the buffalo: "The soldier band went first, riding 20 abreast, and anybody who dared go ahead of them would get knocked off his horse. They kept order, and everybody had to obey. After them came the hunters, riding five abreast. The people came up in the rear." Looking after the hunters, Black Elk noted, was the principal hunt master, or "adviser," who offered instructions to the best young men, noted for their exploits on both the warpath and the hunting ground. "To these he said: 'Good young warriors, my relatives, your work I know is good. What you do is good always; so today you shall feed the helpless. Perhaps there are some old and feeble people without sons, or some who have little children and no man. You shall help these, and whatever you kill shall be theirs.' This was a great honor for the young men."

When the hunters came upon the buffalo herd, they circled the animals in a large surround, said Black Elk, "and the cry went up, as in a battle. 'Hoka Hey!' which meant 'to charge.' Then there was a great dust and everybody shouted and all the hunters went in to kill—every man for himself. They were all nearly naked, with their quivers full of arrows hanging on their left sides, and they would ride right up to a bison and shoot him in the left shoulder. Some of the arrows would go in up to the feathers, and sometimes those that struck no bones went right straight through. Everybody was very happy."

Black Elk described how the people feasted all night long and danced and sang during the joyful get-togethers. As a postscript to his account, he fondly recalled the "war games" that the children played in camp. The object usually was to steal a piece of meat from the grownups without being caught, and Black Elk told how he as a youngster had once attempted the feat himself. "I crawled up to a leaning tree beside a tipi, and there was meat hanging on the limbs. I wanted a tongue I saw up there in the moonlight, so I climbed up. But just as I was about to reach it, the man in the tipi yelled 'Ye-a-a!' He was saying this to his dog, who was stealing some meat, too, but I thought the man had seen me, and I was so scared I fell out of the tree and ran away crying."

Taxidermists for the Kansas Pacific Railway Company pose with their handiwork, a huge display of animal heads and horns, mostly buffalo. The company used the bison as a gimmick to help advertise their railroad.

Eight pairs of buffalo horns in graduated sizes form the legs, arms, and part of the back of this 1890s chair. Such chairs were popular additions to parlors during the early 20th century.

Workers at a railroad siding in Saskatchewan prepare to load huge piles of animal bones, primarily buffalo, onto boxcars for shipment to processing centers. The bones were used in refining sugar and for making buttons, combs, and knife handles.

Black Elk was born in 1863, when millions of buffalo still populated the Plains, and he was raised in the old ways, hunting with bow and arrow, moving from camp to camp with the seasons and the herds. But times were changing rapidly. The first smoke-belching paddle-wheel steamboat had appeared on the Missouri some 30 years before his birth. With such easy, economical transport, whites soon began to traffic widely in buffalo hides. At trading posts along the Missouri and other major rivers of the Plains, Indians exchanged their skins for alluring commodities such as guns, knives, whiskey, coffee, and sugar. As their hankering for these trade goods increased, buffalo hunters no longer limited their take to what they and their families could use. In the late 1830s, George Catlin reported that the Indians already were culling between 150,000 and 200,000 buffalo yearly for their skins alone. That trend was accentuated after the Civil War when the clumsy musket, which some Indians had been using to hunt buffalo, gave way to the repeating rifle. With one of those handy and efficient weapons, a determined man could kill more than 100 buffalo any day, every day.

Before long, railroad lines were fanning out across the Plains, and whites were doing most of the hunting themselves, gunning down entire herds and shipping the skins back east to be processed in tanning plants. These remorseless new hunters pursued their prey without ceremony, nor did they bother to thank the animals for the bounty they offered up. To many Native Americans, who watched in dismay as the buffalo all but vanished from the Plains, it seemed that the creatures had suffered a blow to the spirit that was greater than any wound to the flesh, and that the animals had decided to retreat from a world that no longer honored their life-sustaining power.

The Indians mourned that retreat, and they lamented their own fate as well. By 1885 most of the Plains peoples had been deprived of their essential livelihood and forced onto government reservations. In time, some tribes would reclaim the buffalo, tending small herds and culling them periodically to help nourish the people. In the early days of the reservation era, however, dejected hunters found themselves dependent on government largess. Hoping to alleviate hunger and give the men something to do, United States Indian agents occasionally encouraged them to shoot down with firearms or bows and arrows the cattle that had been collected in corrals for their use. The Indians shrugged and went along with this parody of a piskin. Meat of any kind was welcome, they reasoned. But the thrill of the pursuit was gone. ◆

Oglala Sioux riders drive part of the tribe's buffalo herd toward fences that will funnel them into a corral during the 1992 spring roundup on the Slim Butte Game Range in South Dakota. Each year, the tribe slaughters about 130 animals for ceremonial purposes and to provide fresh meat.

PORTABLE SHELTER FOR ALL SEASONS

Inscribed upon a late-evening sky, the tipis of a Blackfeet encampment in northwestern Montana glow from the light of campfires within. The grazing horses complete a scene of communal tranquillity in this tinted photograph from about 1900.

In 1601 Juan de Oñate, the first European to explore the Great Plains, marveled at the lofty, conic structures he observed there, dwellings that were "built as skillfully as any house in Italy." What the Spaniard saw was the tipi, a tent that had evolved over the centuries into the ideal house for the nomadic tribes of the Plains.

The name *tipi* derives from two Sioux words for an object that is "used to dwell in." Other tribes call the tent a lodge, and the poles that hold it up lodgepoles. No matter what the name, the tipi had many assets for the nomads who followed the buffalo herds. With its thin covering of buffalo hide, it remained cool in the sweltering Plains summers, but insulating cloths made it snug in the blustery winters. Best of all, the tipi could be quickly dismantled and easily transported. When the tribes followed the buffalo, their houses went with them.

For the Indians of the Plains, however, the tipi was more than protection from the elements. The tent was a sanctified place whose circular ground plan echoed the surrounding disk of the earth as it lay beneath the heavens. Its floor represented the earth, its walls the sky. Its poles, as they stretched toward the firmament, were pathways that linked the earthbound people with the Great Spirit who lived on high.

When the days of buffalo hunting ended and reservation life began, the use of the tipi gradually gave way to more permanent housing. But even today, the tipi continues to serve a ceremonial purpose, and many Plains Indians erect a tipi near their homes during the summer months. Like their ancestors, they regard the tipi as a "good mother" who shelters her children.

Assembly of the tipi started with a framework of either three or four primary poles (depending on tribal tradition) made of smoothed pine or red cedar, four inches thick and about 20 feet in length.

Secondary poles were laid in prescribed positions in the crotches of the foundation poles and lashed tight, forming the tipi's egg-shaped base that customarily measured 12 to 20 feet from back to front.

ASSEMBLING THE TIPI

In most Plains tribes, women made the tipis and bore the responsiblity for them. Among their many other duties, women stripped the bark from the lodgepoles, scraped and tanned the hides and sewed them together to make covers, and chose the exact spot on which to raise the tent in the encampment.

Blackfeet women could assemble a tipi in little more than an hour. Although the women usually worked in pairs, a group of friends and relatives might gather to help sew a new tipi cover or to make major repairs to an old one, an occasion that often called for a feast. Once a tipi cover deteriorated beyond repair, it was sectioned for other uses. The dark, smoke-impregnated hide from the top of the tent was particularly waterproof and excellent for making moccasins.

When the time came to strike camp, women dismantled and folded the tipis and lashed them to the travois— A-shaped skids fashioned from lodgepoles and pulled by a dog or a horse. The poles, as heavy as 20 pounds each, were precious on the largely treeless Plains; five of them were worth the price of a horse.

The side of the tipi opposite the opening was erected at a steeper angle to present a stiff spine to the prevailing winds and to increase the available headroom.

A tipi covering was sewn from 12 to 14 buffalo hides or, after herds had been decimated, lighter and more flexible canvas obtained from the government or in trade.

The tipi's smoke hole and ventilator flaps were located on the long, more gently sloping front side in order to avoid the tangle of poles at the apex. The fireplace was offset directly beneath the smoke hole.

While most Plains tipis were covered with unadorned hide or canvas, some were richly decorated for ceremonial use, or to denote membership in a particular clan. This Sioux covering, made about 1830, bears symbols that signify the Sacred Pipe ceremony.

THE FAMILY TENT

Each family tipi was assigned a place in the tribal circle and was further identified by individualized ornament and decorated entrance covers. Etiquette prescribed that visitors enter another's tipi unannounced only if the door flap was open. If the flap was closed, visitors were expected to either call out or cough when approaching, or to use a knocker. A door tied shut with sticks crisscrossing the entrance made it clear that the owner was absent or wished not to be disturbed.

Extra privacy from the gaze of outsiders was provided by interior linings called dew cloths, which gave the tipi a translucent look, softening campfire shadows and minimizing the inhabitants' exposure as targets for enemy attackers.

A tipi door cover created by Crow Indians features painted geometric designs on a 54-by-30-inch rawhide flap that is framed by chokecherry branches.

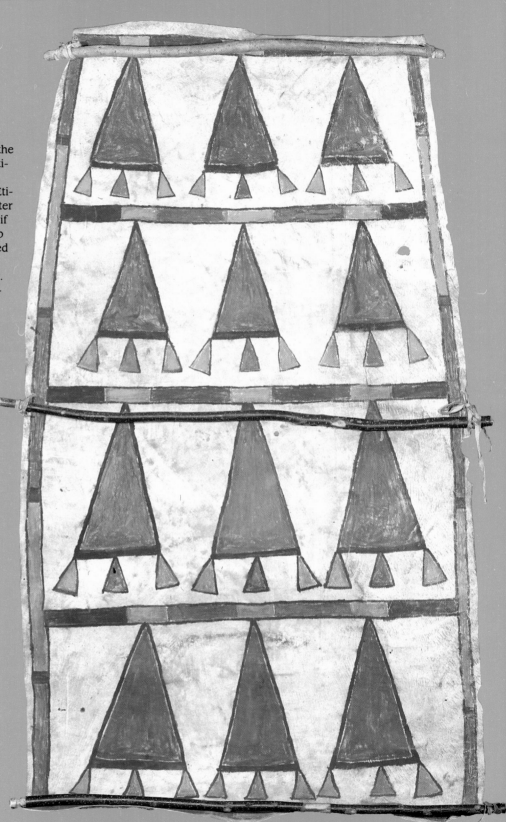

A Cheyenne tipi or-
nament is made of
leather thongs that
have been wrapped
with colored grasses
and then trimmed
with yarn tufts.

In hot weather, the
sides of a tipi could
be rolled up to ad-
mit cooling breezes,
as shown in this
1913 photograph of
a Crow encampment.

A row of wooden
pins could seal a
tipi tight against the
elements, while an
anchoring stake
helped keep the tent
stable in high winds.
Smoke flaps were
adjusted by moving
exterior poles. A
bell signaled a shift
of the wind.

POLES

TIPI ORNAMENT

SMOKE FLAP POLE

SMOKE FLAP

LACING PINS

DOOR KNOCKER

ANCHORING STAKE

DOOR FLAP

PEGS

CUSTOMS OF LIFE IN A LODGE

Everyday life within the tipi was governed by a set of customs. The head of the household always sat in the place of honor, against the wall opposite the entrance. Men generally entered a tipi on the right side of the entrance, women on the left. It was considered poor form to pass between a person and the fire at the tipi's center.

At meals, men were served first, and the host usually waited until his guests had finished eating before partaking himself. Unless they were long-distance travelers, guests were expected to bring their own plates and utensils. Children were to remain quiet while the adults conversed.

BED

ALTAR

FIREPLACE

FIREWOOD

TRIPOD POLE

ENTRANCE

In an average-sized tipi, three fur-covered beds placed along the walls could sleep six people. The bedding was rolled and stored during the day. Weapons and riding gear were kept on the men's side of the tent, while firewood and cooking pots were stored near the door on the women's side.

Ornaments like this woven Cheyenne disk were decorative touches concealing the sections where the tipi's liner was tied to its poles.

In this photograph that was taken in the early 20th century, a Blackfeet chief by the name of Wades in Water and his wife pose in their richly decorated tipi during an encampment near Browning, Montana.

A decorative liner, the dew cloth, helped insulate the tipi by creating a pocket of air that retained heat and prevented condensation. Liners were tied to the lodgepoles about six feet up and anchored with stones.

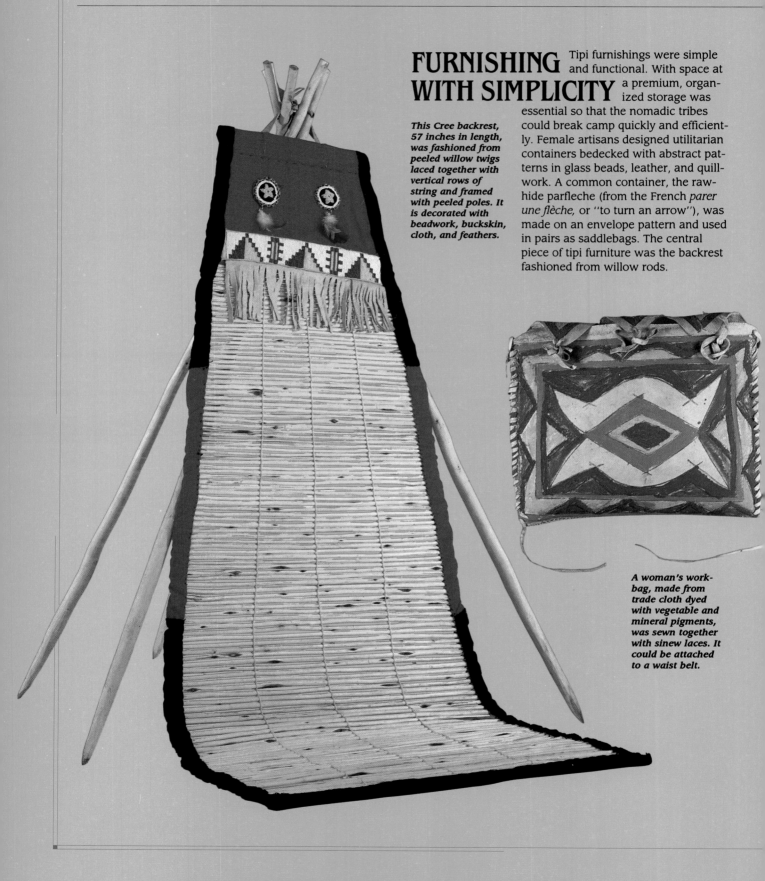

FURNISHING WITH SIMPLICITY

Tipi furnishings were simple and functional. With space at a premium, organized storage was essential so that the nomadic tribes could break camp quickly and efficiently. Female artisans designed utilitarian containers bedecked with abstract patterns in glass beads, leather, and quillwork. A common container, the rawhide parfleche (from the French *parer une flèche,* or "to turn an arrow"), was made on an envelope pattern and used in pairs as saddlebags. The central piece of tipi furniture was the backrest fashioned from willow rods.

This Cree backrest, 57 inches in length, was fashioned from peeled willow twigs laced together with vertical rows of string and framed with peeled poles. It is decorated with beadwork, buckskin, cloth, and feathers.

A woman's work-bag, made from trade cloth dyed with vegetable and mineral pigments, was sewn together with sinew laces. It could be attached to a waist belt.

The quillwork and buckskin "possible bag" was so called because it could contain "every possible thing." The alternating bands produced a striped pattern the Arapaho deemed sacred.

A Blackfeet rawhide medicine bag, circa 1860, stored herbal remedies and sacred objects. The bag was hung over the owner's bed to bring good fortune to the household.

This painted rawhide Lakota clothing trunk was better suited for stacking on wagons than the envelope-style parfleches. Among all the Plains nomads, only the Lakota made such boxes.

TIPIS INSPIRED BY DREAMS

All tipis were sacred to their inhabitants, but some had a special power derived from dreams or visions. Called medicine tipis, they were often painted with images of animals that appeared to a vision seeker and lent him strength. This power was communicated not only by the likeness of the animal on the tipi but also by holy objects stored in a bundle inside or displayed as a flag from the roof, like the stuffed eagle at left, which crowned an eagle tipi of the Blackfoot Confederacy, seen at right. Many of the medicine tipi designs of the Blackfeet originated long ago, but the motifs and the sacred objects associated with them have been faithfully handed down as family keepsakes or as honors to be purchased and prized, with each transfer marked by a special ceremony investing the new owner with the power of the original vision.

Like the designs, the dreams that inspired them have been preserved in tribal lore. These stories and motifs—portrayed on these pages by the Blackfeet artist Victor Pepion—testify to the enduring bond between the people and the creatures around them. As Old Man, the legendary Creator of the Blackfeet, told the first members of the tribe: "Go away by yourself, and go to sleep. Something will come to you in your dream that will help you. It may be some animal. Whatever this animal tells you in your sleep, you must do. Obey it. Be guided by it. If later you want help, if you are traveling alone and cry aloud for help, your prayer will be answered. It may be by the eagles, perhaps by the buffalo, or by the bears. Whatever animal hears your prayer, you must listen to it."

THE EAGLE TIPI

The vision that inspired this medicine tipi was received by a Blackfeet youth named Bad Roads, who went out into the hills with a companion in search of dreams that would make them brave warriors. Bad Roads dreamed of a spirit who invited him into a tipi. "I am the leader of all the eagles," this spirit told him. "When you get home, go out on a high hill and dig a hole deep enough to get into. Lay sticks across the top of the hole you dig. Go kill a calf or rabbit to use as bait, and tie it down so the eagle won't fly away with it. Hide in the hole until one of my children alights there; then catch him by the legs. In that way you can catch an eagle, kill him, tan the skin, and hang him in back of your tipi." In this manner, Bad Roads and his descendants learned to acquire some of the eagle's power by trapping the bird and displaying it from a tipi similar to the one in the dream, showing two eagles facing each other, with constellations in the night sky above and fallen stars amid the hills below.

THE FISH TIPI

This design was bequeathed to a Blackfeet boy named One Spot, who loved to go down to the river and fish. One night as he camped near the river, a spirit appeared to the boy in a dream and invited him to a lodge by the water's edge. "My son," his host said, "I have brought you here to see my tipi. I will give it to you if you won't kill my children, the fish, anymore. You have been killing all of my children. If you take this tipi of mine, you are not supposed to eat fish or kill them." One Spot accepted the offer and took possession of the lodge. Although his people had to give up eating fish, the medicine tipi allowed them to share in the power of the watery creatures, which were esteemed by the Indians for their quickness and deep cunning.

THE HORSE TIPI

A man received this tipi design as a reward for the devotion he showed to a certain buckskin-colored horse, which often visited the man in his dreams and worked wonders for him. When war broke out between the Blackfeet and the Sioux, the man's brother rode this horse into battle, and both rider and horse were wounded. The man sought out his fallen brother and saw that his wound was not serious, but the horse was gravely injured. He put yellow medicine paint on the horse's wounds, but it could not rise. He offered the animal sweet grass and songs, and finally, it stood up and grew strong again. In gratitude, the horse came to the man in a vision and gave him this tipi. It conveyed the power of healing, and the man's curing skills became legend.

THE BUFFALO TIPI

One legend concerning this design tells of a chief who downed a buffalo bull and began to skin it alive, so enraging the animal that it gored him. "My son," the bull told him, "I have done this because you showed me no pity. Also, I want to prove to you my su-pernatural power. You must die from these injuries, but I will give you my power. Your spirit will return to your body if you will fol-low my directions." The chief gave those in-structions to his men, and after he died, they wrapped him in buffalo hide and threw him in the river. As foretold, the chief's spir-it reentered his body, and he walked from the water. Soon he dreamed of the buffalo and learned to paint its medicine tipi, with arrows from the animal's throat and heart signifying the vitality it offered the people.

THE OTTER TIPI

This medicine came to a man named Big Snake as he was leading people across the Missouri River. His followers warned him that the river would swallow him if he waded across, but Big Snake ignored them. As he reached midstream, he went under, and his wife, looking on from the near bank, began chanting his death song. At last, he surfaced at the far bank, carrying an otter he had killed with his knife after it grabbed his legs and pulled him down. That night, the animal's spirit spoke to him in a dream. "I wanted to take you down to my tipi. Since you have my pelt, I have come to give you my tipi anyway." Thus, Big Snake inherited the painted Otter Tipi and flew its pelt from the roof to show that he had braved the depths and claimed the animal's power.

4

A medicine wheel, a circle in stone 70 feet across and dating from about 1700, crowns a plateau in the Bighorn Mountains of Wyoming. Scattered throughout the northwestern Plains, such ceremonial sites reflect the reverence in which all Indians hold the shape of the circle—a sentiment expressed domestically by camp circles such as the village of the Awatixa Indians (top), a branch of the Hidatsa tribe.

THE TIMELESS CYCLE OF CEREMONY

They gathered in warm weather. After going their separate ways for most of the year, the nomadic bands began arriving at the annual tribal assembly during the summer. Under the supervision of camp police from the warrior societies, the new campsite bustled with energy. For days and sometimes weeks, people and animals converged from all directions. Streams of travois, drawn by horse or dog, arrived, and the poles and tipi covers were unloaded. The horses were put out to pasture on the fresh summer grass, and the lodges went up, many of them brilliantly decorated with painted war honors and sacred symbols. An enormous encampment gradually took shape. At dusk, it was a breathtaking sight visible from miles away, with campfires flickering and tipis illuminated from within, glowing ghostlike against the darkening prairie sky. Each band had its assigned place. When the camp was completed, it consisted of a series of concentric rings that might contain hundreds of tipis. The entire gathering took the form of a giant circle up to one mile in diameter.

The camp circle was a fitting symbol. To the Sioux, Cheyenne, and other nomads of the Plains, who gathered each summer during the glory days of the 19th century, the circle was a sacred image, the symbol of harmony, unity, and wholeness. "The sun and the sky, the earth and the moon are round like a shield," an Oglala Sioux elder once explained. "Everything that breathes is round like the body of a man. Everything that grows from the ground is round like the stem of a tree. For these reasons, the Oglala make their tipis circular, their camp circular, and sit in a circle in all ceremonies." The formation of the annual camp circle, with an opening facing east toward the rising sun, thus was intended to reaffirm the political and spiritual unity of the nation—to renew the people's connection with one another and with the universe.

All summer, the great gathering buzzed with activity. Here, the people organized the communal buffalo hunt and socialized with relatives and friends they had not seen in nine or 10 months. The elders transacted tribal political business; the young raced horses and pressed courtships. Warriors proudly recounted coups scored in combat; the storytellers passed on the ancient traditions of the tribe. Above all, the encampment echoed with the music, chants, and dancing of the tribe's abundant repertoire of rituals and religious ceremonies.

While central to the lives of virtually all Native Americans, ceremonial events particularly flourished on the Plains. For one thing, the bountiful harvests of buffalo that were made possible by the introduction of the horse afforded these tribes ample leisure time for public ritual. In addition, the months spent hunting in small groups sharpened the nomads' appetites for elaborate costumed ceremonies involving hundreds of participants. The unvarying structure of these rituals, along with the social interaction that occurred between the various clans and other tribal associations, reinforced old friendships and brought reassurance and stability to the uncertain lives of the Indians.

The rituals fulfilled a variety of purposes. Some of them marked a young person's coming of age or initiation into adulthood. Others celebrated a victory in battle or the taking of an enemy scalp. And some served merely to entertain. But most were religious rites, aimed at communicating with the spirit world so that the nation might live and continue to flourish. The most spectacular of these rituals was the Sun Dance, an exhausting ceremony lasting up to 12 days that typically culminated the summer encampment.

The ceremonies were filled with music and dancing. Chanting a cycle

A Blackfeet man's fringed buckskin shirt, decorated with porcupine quills worked into geometric bands, invested its wearer with potent medicine for ceremonial occasions. The deer hides used to make such shirts were cut as little as possible to demonstrate respect for the animal and to retain its power for the wearer. The shirt's fringes represent a connection to the Great Spirit. Locks of human hair attached across the breast—either taken in battle or donated by friend or relative—celebrated success in battle.

of traditional verses, shaking rattles made of buffalo hoofs or gourds filled with pebbles or seeds, blowing whistles fashioned from eagle bones, pounding on rawhide drums—all helped generate the spiritual power that Indians called "medicine." The drum especially was "the pulse," as the great Oglala Sioux holy man Black Elk put it, "the heart, throbbing at the center of the universe." But it was the dance—the intricate whirling and kaleidoscopic blur of painted and feathered bodies—that combined these elements into the prayerful soul of Plains ritual.

"Dancing is one of the principal and most valued amusements of the Indian, and much more frequently practiced by them than by any civilized society," wrote George Catlin, the Philadelphia lawyer and painter who traveled extensively among the Plains tribes during the 1830s and faithfully recorded their way of life. "Instead of the 'giddy maze' of the quadrille or the country dance, enlivened by the cheering smiles and graces of silken beauty, the Indian performs his rounds with jumps and starts, and yells, much to the satisfaction of his own exclusive self, and infinite amusement of the gentler sex, who are always looking on, but seldom allowed so great a pleasure, or so signal an honor, as that of joining with their lords in this or any other entertainment."

Catlin, who spent much of his time with Mandan farmers on the upper Missouri River, could attest that ritualism thrived even in the permanent villages on the fringes of the Plains. Except during their periodic buffalo hunts, the Mandan, the Hidatsa, the Pawnee, and other seminomadic tribes lived together, and their gatherings took place inside their cozy villages rather than in the great summer circle camps that dominated the yearly cycle of other Plains tribes. They staged public rituals to coincide with significant events in the village calendar, focusing their rounds of ceremonies equally on the two pursuits that sustained them: farming and the buffalo. Among the Mandan and the Hidatsa, for example, the arrival of the first migratory water birds in late spring signaled the start of dances intended to make the corn grow. Then, following the harvest festivals in the fall, the villagers turned their attention to honoring the buffalo spirits.

As the farming people rode their newly acquired horses onto the Plains in search of the buffalo, they encountered the hunting tribes. The two groups adopted many of each other's rituals, while continuing to practice their own. As a result, ceremonies varied from tribe to tribe. Many of these were based on the theme of warfare. Summer encampment afforded an opportunity for warriors to parade the symbols of their valor before

Sacred to the Blackfeet, Blood, and Piegan Indians, Montana's Chief Mountain soars 9,080 feet above sea level, making it visible anywhere in Blackfeet territory. According to Blackfeet legend, the mountain was the only land left unsubmerged after a great flood covered the earth. From that spot, the Creator, Old Man, made the present earth.

the entire tribe. They wore eagle feather bonnets or porcupine quills wrapped around their scalp lock and other finery of the warrior's craft, regaled tribe members with tales of their heroism, and staged special dances associated with the warpath.

During the 19th century, for example, encampments of the Piegan branch of the Blackfoot Confederacy featured a spectacular ceremony that originated as a prelude to a scalp-raiding party. Known as the Riding Big or Horse Dance, it began with the warriors riding out from camp to a nearby ridge. There they donned war paint and costumes, daubed their horses with symbols of their war exploits, decorated them with masks and bells, and tied feathers in their tails. The warriors then remounted and converged upon the camp from the four points of the compass as if attacking an enemy stronghold. In the center of the camp stood their reception committee—a group of old men and women beating drums and singing. The warriors circled the camp, brandishing their weapons, and then dismounted and engaged in mock combat. At last they began dancing on foot to the rhythm of the drums, imitating the gait of their horses prancing along beside them.

Summer encampment was the occasion for members of the warrior societies to convene and dispose of societal business during a series of public rituals. One all-too-frequent task was the replacement of officers who had been killed in battle. In the Kit Fox Society of the Crow, members erected two large tipis in the center of the camp. They assembled there, rolling up the sides of the tipis so that the rest of the tribe could view the ceremony. In one of the tipis, in front of a rack that displayed the society's paraphernalia, three elders responsible for selecting the new officers sat cross-legged on the ground.

A singer began the traditional chant honoring the fallen comrade by intoning, "One of the Foxes did not return." To this slow rhythm, the three old men arose and danced, uttering dirgelike war cries. Then two of them picked up a ceremonial pipe and carried it to one of the young men they had chosen as a new officer. The ceremony was repeated until all of the offices had been filled. The old men instructed the new officers in their duties, and then an aging former officer might address them. He would grasp one of the lances of office and, after describing his own war exploits, return the lance by jabbing it into the ground in front of the new owner, who took hold of it. A feast of boiled puppy, accompanied by additional dances and songs, brought the celebration to a close.

Equally elaborate ceremonies marked the initiation of new members into the warrior societies. Among the Sioux, young men marked for induction into the Kit Fox Society shaved their heads and were marshaled into the initiation ceremony by two Kit Foxes brandishing medicine whips that conferred a special power on the warriors; those same whips would later be wielded ceremonially to banish the inductees if they showed cowardice in battle or broke the society's rules. During their initiation, the men with shaved heads sat by the Drum Keeper, whose instrument was decorated with eagle feathers and enemy scalps, among other talismans. Striking a membrane of deer hide stretched over a hollow cottonwood log, the Drum Keeper set the pace for the songs and dances at this and other rites of the society. As befitted an organization whose activities in war and in peace were characterized by strict discipline, the two men with whips sometimes prowled the periphery of the dance circle, keeping the men in a tight bunch.

During the initiation rites of the Braves Society of the Blackfeet, which were performed around a large lodge constructed in the center of the camp, participants wore bear and coyote skins and painted themselves in many colors and designs. They shot arrows over the heads of the onlookers, tracked the arrows down, and then marched back into camp chanting the society's song. It was their privilege to confiscate any food they saw—even victuals cooking in the kettle—and take it back to their lodge for a night of feasting.

In sharp contrast to the solemnity of most Plains ceremonies were the public antics of the sacred clowns, known as contraries. Called *heyoka* among the Sioux and *hohnuhk'e* among the Cheyenne, the contraries were known for their practice of saying and doing everything in reverse. The contrary signified his assent by saying no, sat his horse backward, and when told to go away, came nearer. At circle camp, contraries worked together to furnish comic relief. They undertook stunts such as throwing boiling water on one another's hands, then complaining of the cold (their hands having been protected from scalding by a coating of plant extract). For all their absurdity, however, contraries were highly valued members of their communities. They had not adopted their outlandish behavior on a whim, but came to it by sacred obligation. Contraries were Thunder Dreamers—men and, very rarely, women who took up their calling after a dream or a vision involving thunder and lightning. They were also highly valued as warriors because they would fight valiantly when the battle seemed most hopeless.

The Sioux believe that contraries get their power from the Wakinyan, or "Thunderbirds," the enormous winged creatures who live with their young on a mountain high above the clouds. According to Sioux legend, the thunder resounds when the thunderbirds open their beaks to speak, and lightning flashes when they open their eyes. From time to time, the thunderbirds send a dream to a human being and appoint that person to do their work on earth. The contrary behaves as he does because the thunderbird power, like thunder and lightning, involves opposites—heat and cold, fire and ice. Consequently, while a contrary's actions were always ridiculous and often shameful, he himself was a respected visionary who performed a spiritual service for the tribe. "The heyoka presents the truth of his vision through comic actions," explained Black Elk, "the idea being that the people should be put in a happy, jolly frame of mind before the great truth is presented."

Brave Wolf, a Cheyenne, had always been afraid of thunder until a dream revealed to him that he would lose this fear if he became a contrary. He then used eight horses along with other valuables to purchase from one of the tribe's two or three contraries the special lance that symbolized the role. For about 10 years, Brave Wolf bore the strange lance, which was shaped like a bow with two strings, and faithfully carried out his duties as a contrary until another member of the tribe lifted his burden by purchasing the lance after he, too, dreamed of thunder.

Although his fellow tribesmen typically regarded a contrary with a mixture of awe and amusement, his lot was arduous, and few Indians wished to play the role all their lives. A Cheyenne hohnuhk'e, for example, was obliged to paint himself red and live alone, usually on a distant hilltop. He was not allowed to joke except as part of the public amusement. A Sioux heyoka had to dress in rags and constantly talk in a senseless manner. But their antics were so popular and their bravery in battle so valued that several tribes maintained contrary societies—known to the Crow and the Arapaho as Crazy Dogs. Their members played the fool in rituals, but fought with uncommon ferocity.

Plains Indians also found entertainment of an unintended kind in the public demonstrations of the medicine men. Sometimes referred to as shamans or priests, these personages possessed a special link with the spirit world that they put to use either in healing or in the conduct of all manner of rituals—and occasionally in both spheres. Even though their duties normally required serious attention to supernatural business, they often relaxed at circle camp by indulging in contests with one another to prove their prowess. The competition typically consisted of displays of

At Montana's Fort Belknap Reservation in 1906, the chief of the Fool Society of the Assiniboin tosses a piece of liver—an organ normally respected for its special qualities—to the other members of his group. The masks they are wearing mark them as contraries, clowns who amuse and instruct their fellow tribesmen by behaving in a manner counter to accepted social norms.

conjuring and feats of hypnotic self-control such as walking barefoot through a fire. Spectators might roar with derision at the failed powers of those shamans who came off second best, but it was no laughing matter for the holy man, who could lose his prestige and even his high position.

More important than public amusements, warrior society rites and other essentially secular practices were the ceremonial expressions of religious beliefs. Like native societies throughout North America, Plains peoples adhered to the conviction that spiritual power was a part of everyday life. Thus, all elements of life, even inanimate objects such as stones or mountains, could be infused with sacred power. Most tribes believed that this power derived from the original Creator. While not limited to any sin-

Members of the Crow Tobacco Society engage in a springtime ceremony to induct new participants into the group. Atop the altar before the drummers are an eagle wing and pelts used in their dances. An ancient Crow prophecy says that when the sacred tobacco is gone, "then finally it will be the end of time and the world will end."

gle divine being, this cosmic power often had a name. The Blackfeet used the term Old Man, the Crow referred to Old Man Coyote as a creator, and the Sioux termed the power Wakan Tanka, or "Great Mystery." Divine power resided everywhere. It could be found in human achievement and rarely was farther away than the wind or the nearest rock or tree.

On the Plains, religious rites served both to express these convictions and to enlist the help of the ubiquitous supernatural forces. In the rich, symbolic panoply of the region's ceremonies, cosmic power enabled animals to talk and stones to influence people. Deities inhabited the thunder and the wind, roaring and dancing overhead. All of the ceremonial components—the body paint, the drumbeats, the dancing, the communal spirit of a large gathering—dramatized the presence of spiritual power and ensured that the power would be passed from generation to generation. At the same time, the rituals evoked the cosmic powers to restore harmony and balance among community members and to provide protection against misfortune. Invoked by ceremony, a tribe's spiritual medicine could keep it safe and healthy in a dangerous environment.

Most ceremonies were elaborately staged and required the participation of many members of the tribe. Shamans usually directed them to make certain that the rites were performed in precisely the right manner; lapses in procedure, it was believed, not only would result in failure to produce the desired end but might actually bring about harm. The power of the shaman to serve as an intermediary between the supernatural and ordinary tribe members typically derived from a dream, vision, or other unique experience that pierced the boundary between the everyday world and the spiritual forces that surround it. Those so honored sometimes grouped together in special dream cults and spoke in tongues unintelligible to laymen. Shamans were almost always men, although some women qualified—especially postmenopausal women no longer subject to the menstrual taboo that barred most females from ceremonial roles.

One ritual that combined both sacred and social activities was the Crow Tobacco Society adoption ceremony. Although they were nonagricultural nomads, the Crow, like the Blackfeet and the Sarsi, cultivated a special kind of tobacco that was never smoked, even on the most sacred occasions, but was raised solely for spiritual and ceremonial reasons. According to tribal legend, the Creator gave the seeds to the Crow chief, No Vitals. As custodians of the tradition, members of the Tobacco Society planted the seeds during an annual spring rite, danced to make them grow faster, and, after harvest, spread the stems and leaves upon the wa-

Marking the site as sacred, petroglyphs were inscribed on a slab of rock (left) at the Minnesota quarry where for centuries Indians have come to obtain the soft red stone used to make prized pipe bowls, like the examples pictured here. (The bowl on the Sioux pipe above is painted.) The quarry, which is believed to be imbued with special powers, has always been regarded as nontribal territory, where all Indians have been able to procure pipestone in peace. The stone acquired the name catlinite in the 1800s after artist George Catlin brought it to the attention of white America.

ters of a creek or river and preserved the seeds for planting the next spring. Their activities celebrated the original gift of the tobacco plant and renewed the ties that bound all Crow peoples together. So great was the desire to become a member—and so diverse the visions and dreams that inspired activities—that the Tobacco Society eventually subdivided into no fewer than 30 different chapters.

Membership in a chapter was attained through a process of ritual adoption and purchase. A vow frequently initiated the process: A man might pledge to join if his ill relative recovered, or a young couple might make the vow to become members if their sick child lived. It was commonly believed that failure to fulfill the vow would bring sickness or misfortune. Chapters also recruited potential members—usually couples—with gifts and feasting. Chapter members agreed to serve as sponsors, or ritual parents, teaching novices the songs and dances necessary for their participation in the adoption ceremony. Gifts flowed both ways in this relationship, although it was understood that the "parents" were to receive the lion's share of them. Both sponsors and novices committed themselves to an enduring relationship of mutual support that extended the individual's range of natural kinship.

The high point of the Tobacco Society calendar was the adoption ceremony held each summer, midway between the planting and the harvesting of the sacred tobacco plants. After several Crow bands had gathered together, a special tipi was erected that contained an unusual altar consisting of a rectangular plot of cleared ground bordered by willow arches and covered with rows of juniper sprigs. This shrine conveyed an image of fertility in keeping with the Tobacco Society's emphasis on the annual renewal of nature and of the social world. Rolled-up side covers permit-

ted other members of the tribe to witness the daylong rites of singing, drumming, dancing, and feasting.

During the ceremony, the actual families of the novices presented the adopters—the ritual families—with clothing and other valuable gifts. Even the designs that decorated the faces of participants were frequently exchanged. The particular designs had been inspired by individual visions or dreams and, therefore, were considered personal property. An initiate who wanted to use the design was required to either pay the owner for the privilege, in effect buying the vision that had inspired it, or else receive it free as a token of affection.

An essential element in virtually all of the religious ceremonies performed by the Plains Indians was the act of smoking a sacred pipe. The pipe served as a kind of portable altar for the offering of tobacco smoke as a sacrifice to the spirit world. The Sioux, the Arapaho, the Gros Ventre, and other Plains tribes each possessed a sacred pipe that they traced back to their creation legends. For the Cree, this pipe was a parting gift from the Creator. For the Sioux, it was the legacy of White Buffalo Calf Woman, the beautiful maiden of their most significant legend. She gave them not only the pipe but also the Seven Rites that constitute the heart of their tribal ritual; then she forged their symbolic link with all four-legged creatures by transforming herself into a white buffalo calf.

"The most sacred thing we have is the Holy Pipe," Miniconjou Sioux John Lame Deer said. "Its red stone is our flesh and blood. It is our heart. In its bowl is the whole universe. Every grain of tobacco represents a living thing. When you hold the pipe, you can speak nothing but the truth." Ornately designed and elaborately decorated replicas of these sacred pipes—some of them up to five feet long—served the people of the Plains on numerous occasions. Filled with kinnikinnick, an aromatic mixture of tobacco and various herbs, and ignited with a burning buffalo chip, the pipe helped sanctify all aspects of tribal life, including the decision to make war or to end it—hence the phrase "peace pipe" popular among non-Indians. At the summer encampments, Native Americans performed ancient pipe rituals that may well have originated before the birth of Christ.

Although the precise details of pipe rituals varied from tribe to tribe, certain features remained constant. For example, because the stem was considered symbolically male and the bowl symbolically female, they were kept separate until just before the ceremony; joining them made the pipe potent again. Participants sat in a sacred circle and passed the pipe clockwise, the presumed direction of the sun's travel. Before taking a puff, each smoker pointed with the pipe, offering its curl of smoke to sky and earth and to the four cardinal directions.

Another indispensable element in Plains rituals was the saunalike structure known to whites as the sweat lodge. Just as smoke spiraling from the pipe carried special symbolic meaning for the Indians, so too did the steam rising when the red-hot stones inside the lodge were sprayed with water. The act of undergoing heat and steam—known to the Sioux as Inikagapi, or "Taking a Sweat"—was considered a necessary rite of purification before participation in any major ceremony. According to George Sword, an Oglala Sioux, the sweat lodge cleansed both body and mind, sweeping away "all that makes him tired, or all that causes disease, or all that causes him to think wrong."

Every detail of the sweat lodge's construction process reflected the rich spiritual symbolism of the structure. Four or five feet high and shaped

Crow medicine man Tom Yellowtail blesses the framework of a sweat lodge in the Black Canyon Basin of the Bighorn Mountains. Constructed, in the traditional Crow fashion, of 12 bent saplings, the lodge is sited in such a way that its door faces east, toward the rising sun. Typically, sweat lodges are located alongside a river or creek.

At the end of a sweat lodge ceremony conducted by Tom Yellowtail in the summer of 1992, participants bathe in nearby Owl Creek. "After we have rinsed ourselves, we are finished with the sweat lodge ordeal," explained the medicine man in his 1991 autobiography. "It is Nature's way that was given to the Indians a long time ago."

like a dome to represent the universe, it was customarily made of bent willow saplings—a deciduous tree that demonstrated Nature's birth and renewal—and covered with buffalo hides. A hole was dug in the center to receive the hot stones, and the excavated dirt was strewn as a sacred path leading from the opening of the dome to the exterior fireplace, symbolizing the sun, where the stones would be heated. With its warm, dark, and cramped interior and its narrow opening, the sweat lodge was intended to convey a womblike ambiance from which participants would emerge feeling as though they had been born anew. Even the precise numbers of heated rocks and saplings in the structure sometimes possessed symbolic significance for a particular tribe.

About a half-dozen men or women could "take a sweat" at the same time, although not among tribes such as the Blackfeet, who excluded females from the sweat lodge. Occupants sat naked or crouched on pads of sweet-smelling sage. The hot stones were brought in on wooden paddles or deer antlers, and after prayers and chanting, water was sprinkled on them. As the rocks hissed and the steam rose, the pipe might be lighted and passed around the circle, its aroma mixing with the fragrance of the sage. The round of prayers, steam, and smoke would then be repeated. The Sioux, as they did in most ceremonies, punctuated each round of the sweat ritual by crying out their litany, *mitak oays'in'*—"all my relations"—in affirmation of their kinship to all creatures. After a designated number of repetitions, the participants emerged, physically and spiritually revived.

Both smoking and sweating figured in numerous religious ceremonies, including the so-called pledged or vowed dance. This sort of dance was staged at the instigation of an individual, usually a warrior, who vowed to sponsor it in return for divine protection. The vow was usually made in perilous circumstances such as during a battle. Survival meant paying his spiritual debt by organizing the dance, performing in it, furnishing the food for the accompanying feast, and providing gifts for the instructor who oversaw the rituals.

Such a warrior in the Gros Ventre tribe might select from a repertoire of a half-dozen different sacred dances. The dances were ranked in priority, however; the young beginner had to pledge the short and simple one-day Fly Dance, which took its name from the buzzing sound made by dancers at the end, before he could vow to hold the longer and more elaborate affairs, such as the Drum, Dog, and Crazy dances. The vower recruited members of his warrior society age group to help build the ceremonial lodge in the center of the camp circle and to join him in the dance. He also chose a crier—usually a man gifted in oratory—to spread the news to tribal members, all of whom were required to attend the ceremony. Most important, the vower and the other dancers each chose an older man who had already performed the dance to serve as a ritual grandfather. These "grandfathers" helped prepare the ceremony by instructing the dancers in the precise details.

The four days of the prestigious Crazy Dance included at least two daunting features. Along with performing such familiar contrary actions as talking backward, participants had to jump barefoot into the fire, albeit after daubing their feet with protective balm. Another stressful aspect of the dance was the severe test of marital fidelity that occurred during one night of the ceremony. Custom dictated that each participant's wife lie naked with her husband's ritual grandfather in the darkness outside the camp circle. The grandfather was required to touch his lips to hers and pass into her mouth the medicinal plant root he had been chewing. This exercise tested not only the sexual restraint of wife and grandfather but also the nerve of the warrior. Whatever mental anguish he suffered about his wife's potential infidelity was intended as a sacrifice to the spirits.

Sioux women celebrate a battlefield victory with the Scalp Dance, traditionally performed by the female relatives of slain warriors. An enemy's hand, foot, and scalp hang from the center pole; scalps dangle from upheld lances. "Kills and comes back, this is the way the Tetons dance for it," reads the inscription by the artist, Oglala chronicler Amos Bad Heart Bull, who began making such drawings in the late 19th century.

Some men refused to take part in the Crazy Dance rather than suffer through the ordeal of not knowing what their spouses might do. "The husband," recalled a Gros Ventre named Matilda Cuts the Rope, "would have to be a man of strong heart." Tribal lore had it that the penalties for failing the fidelity test could be severe. One ritual grandfather who succumbed to temptation was found dead in his bed four days later.

Far less traumatic were the two vowed dances reserved by the Gros Ventre for the aging members of their tribe. The Old Men's Dance and the Old Women's Dance took place outside the limelight, in lodges beyond the camp circle. Unlike the other sacred dances, where warrior society members enforced attendance, these ceremonies attracted few spectators. Only those members of the tribe considered past the prime of life—men and women in their late forties or older—participated. In both dances, the performers impersonated buffalo with the goal of luring the herds closer to camp in order to make the job of the hunters easier. These dances served the function of making older people feel useful. The male participants graduated into the ranks of "retired old men," a standing that gave them greater freedom to disregard their manners and to talk vulgarly in public. No such license was granted "retired old women."

Among the most important religious rituals on the Plains were those relating to the collections of sacred objects called medicine bundles. The
concept probably originated in the farming villages where certain objects
were thought to bring divine blessings on crops and community members. Consisting of ornaments, dried plants, and preserved animal parts
commonly wrapped in cloth or some creature's skin, the bundle bore
deep symbolic meaning and was intended to bring good fortune. The
contents of personal bundles maintained by individuals reflected their
dreams or visions; white beads, for example, symbolized the hailstones in
a dream of a thunderstorm, and the bundle's otter skin represented water. While similar in form, communal bundles embodied the larger con-
cerns of a clan, society, or tribe. Objects in the communal bundle almost
always could be traced to the people's beliefs about their origins. These
objects and what they symbolized were so intimately bound up in creation stories that many tribes, such as the Cheyenne, considered their
very existence inseparable from that of the bundle.

The rituals connected to the communal bundle spoke to the tribe with
extraordinary resonance. Since bundles were rarely opened for public
view, the ritual act of merely unwrapping such sacrosanct objects and

*The Beggars Dance of the Teton Sioux,
painted in the 1830s by George Catlin, was
held in order to encourage well-off members
of the community to share their bounty with
the less fortunate. Dancers moved through
the village, planting a begging stick (inset)
at selected tipi doorways and singing to the
occupants in order to solicit donations.*

then covering them again—accompanied by prayer, song, and movement that dramatized the creation legends—reinforced the tribe's sense of identity. Bundle ceremonies served to mark special occasions and to propitiate the spirits before an important undertaking such as a hunt or a war party. The Crow Indians, in keeping with their position as a relatively small group attempting to defend their rich hunting grounds in present-day Montana and Wyoming, maintained bundles and performed rituals associated with warfare. The bundles and rituals of the village-dwelling Mandan, on the other hand, focused on such endeavors as growing corn and trapping catfish.

Among the circumstances that called for ceremonies was the transfer of the bundle from one keeper to another. Although maintained for the collective benefit of the community, the tribal bundle was often privately owned and hence subject to purchase and family inheritance—but a burden nonetheless. In addition to performing public rites with the help of his wife, the keeper was required to meet the obligations that were imposed by a host of taboos. In many tribes, he had to keep the bundle suspended from a tripod, making certain it never touched the ground. He might also have to move it several times a day so that it always faced the sun, the presumed source of its power.

All the same, bundle keeping was undeniably prestigious and sometimes profitable. Among the Mandan, ritualistic lore was a proprietary secret, and anyone seeking knowledge of it had to pay the bundle keeper. In the Hidatsa tribe, the keeper could sell the right to perform dances, songs, and prayers that summoned the bundle's spiritual power—but only three times. A fourth sale cost the keeper the right to perform the rituals himself.

Not surprisingly, given its ritual significance, the pipe served as the centerpiece in a number of tribal bundles. The Blackfeet bundle pipe, it was said, derived from Thunder, who had commanded, ''Now, when I first come in the spring, you shall fill and light this pipe, and you shall pray to me, you and the people.'' The pipe bundle was opened at the first rumble of thunder in the spring and in response to vows taken requesting Thunder's intercession to ward off danger. Such bundles proliferated over the years to accommodate the many bands and tribal divisions of the Blackfoot Confederacy. By the l870s, the Blackfeet possessed a score of sacred pipe bundles, the other contents of which varied according to the visions of the different owners.

The Arapaho considered their pipe bundle so sacred that it could not be borne on horseback but had to be carried on foot by the keeper or his wife. When the tribe formed a circle camp, a large ceremonial tipi was constructed in the center to house the bundle and its keeper.

Instead of a pipe, four Sacred Arrows formed the core of the Cheyenne's main bundle. In the legend that related the origins of the tribe, the hero known as Sweet Medicine traveled to a distant mountain where the Creator gave him the arrows. Highly ornate, draped with eagle wing feathers painted red and black and decorated with symbols of the sun, moon, stars, and earth, the arrows were wrapped in the skin of a red fox. Two of the arrows gave the Cheyenne power over other men, the other two gave them power over animals. Along with the bundle, Sweet Medicine handed down commandments on how to live, everything from a proscription against eating raw meat to the sanctity of the number four.

The keeper of the Sacred Arrows occupied an influential position in Cheyenne society. Along with having to pay rigorous attention to various taboos, he was obliged to ritually scar his own flesh as a sacrificial offering. He had to carve the symbolic number four on numerous parts of his body, and a pattern of stripes was cut up the arms, over the shoulders, and down the chest to the sternum, converging under a gouged-out sun and crescent moon.

The bundle was customarily unveiled and renewed when the tribe was threatened by enemies or by natural forces such as a famine. The ceremony typically resulted from a vow taken by an individual, who then visited all 10 bands of the tribe to inform them the event would be held at summer encampment—perhaps on the longest day of the year. It was such a momentous occasion that attendance was mandatory even though many components of the four-day ceremony took place only in the company of priests in a lodge put up in the center of the camp circle. To symbolize the renewal of tribal unity and purpose, the Sacred Arrows were refurbished with new feathers and given any other necessary repairs.

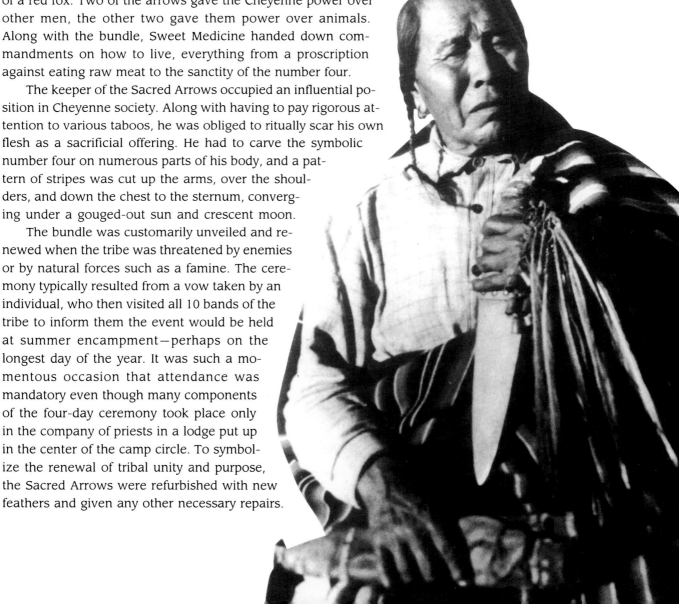

A Blood Indian named Four Bears holds a bear knife, a weapon invested with such powerful medicine that its owner was believed to be immune from arrows, and enemies were said to collapse at its very sight. The owners of these potent knives were obliged to use no other weapon in battle.

The Blackfeet Bear Knife, with its eagle feather pendant, is the focal point of a medicine bundle that includes bear jaws and other potent objects. Owners of such bundles acquired them by undergoing a grueling ritual that involved being pierced with thorns and having to catch the unsheathed knife barehanded when it was thrown.

Women were not only excluded from the ceremony—on the grounds that Sweet Medicine went to the mountain unaccompanied by a mate—but actually confined to their own tipis during the renewal rites. On the final day, every Cheyenne male in camp, even the youngest, was permitted to view the refurbished arrows. The ceremony included other rites to honor the entire family, females as well as males. The shamans prepared willow sticks, each representing a particular family, and passed them through the smoke of incense fires as a blessing.

In the Pawnee villages of present-day Nebraska, practically all ritual life revolved around sacred bundles. In addition to the bundles kept by the larger Pawnee bands, each village had its own, symbolizing the power either of a star or of an animal associated with its oldest legends. The village chief owned the bundle by virtue of his position as direct descendant of the community's legendary founder. Most bundles had similar contents—usually a pipe, tobacco, paint, ears of corn, the skins of various birds and animals, and a preserved human scalp or two. What most differentiated the bundles were the ceremonies related to each one. These observances were part of a busy schedule of rituals that began in the spring and concluded in the fall.

The most remarkable of the bundle rites, the ritual of the morning star (the planet Mars), occurred at infrequent intervals. The prerequisite to the ceremony was the conjunction of two events: A member of the Skidi band of the Pawnee had to dream of the morning star—or a personification of it—and subsequently arise from sleep to actually see the planet coming up over the eastern horizon. The dreamer would then go, in tears, to consult with the priest of the morning star bundle. As soon as he saw the man crying, the priest would put his arm around him, and he, too, would break down. The two men cried because they were obligated to do what the morning star commanded even though both of them knew that it was wrong: They had to sacrifice a human being.

Pawnee tradition dictated that the sacrificial offering for the Morning Star ceremony be a young maiden from the village of a neighboring tribe. The dreamer, outfitted with paint and other regalia from the sacred bundle, including thongs to bind the wrists of the captive, led an expedition of volunteers in search of a 13-year-old girl. Every step of the way was governed by ceremonial rules that prescribed when to sing and dance and the precise manner in which they were to capture the girl. After the girl was brought back to the Pawnee village, the priest watched the sky. When he saw the morning star begin to rise, the four-day ritual, with its mournful litany of 21 songs, commenced.

On the fourth day, shortly before dawn, the priest led a procession of tribe members to the scaffold that had been erected for the rite. The maiden, only now becoming aware of her fate, was coaxed to mount the scaffold where she was tied facing east. As the morning star rose higher, one man rushed up and shot an arrow into her heart; another man cut her breast with a flint knife and daubed her blood on his face. Dried buffalo meat was placed under the scaffold to be consecrated by her dripping blood and then burned as an offering to the morning star.

Every male in the village then came forward to fire arrows into the back of the lifeless maiden; the mothers of boys too small to take part in the ritual fired little arrows for them. Four men carried the body out onto the prairie, laid it facedown, facing the morning star, and sang over and over again, "The earth you shall become a part of." Then they returned to the feasting and dancing in the village, where the bundle of the morning star, wrapped again in its buffalo skins, would await another dream.

Like her father, Cheyenne medicine bundle keeper Josephine Head Swift Limpy tends one of her tribe's two most powerful bundles, Is'siwun—"Sacred Buffalo Hat"—believed to contain the promise of abundance and renewal. Each day, the keeper makes a tobacco offering to the bundle, and every morning and night, she strikes the tipi pole four times in order to announce the opening and closing of Is'siwun's home.

For the great majority of the Plains tribes, the ceremony that ranked supreme among all religious rituals was the Sun Dance. The name came from the Sioux rites that were known as Wi Wanyang Wacipi, or "Gazing at the Sun." White men applied it not only to the Sioux but also to the similar ceremony that other tribes called the Medicine Lodge. Under these or other names, the event was the pinnacle of worship at the summer encampment. Largely a composite that blended elements of other ceremonies with spectacular features of its own, the typical Sun Dance lasted at least eight days and demanded feats of endurance and offerings of excruciating self-torture.

The Sun Dance most likely evolved from simpler ceremonies, probably on the northeastern Plains. The ritual attained its highest complexity among the Arapaho, the Cheyenne, and the Oglala Sioux, groups prominent in that region during the 18th century, and may have originated with one of these nomadic tribes. Even the village dwellers in the area, the Hidatsa and the Mandan, observed their own variants.

As a consequence of the burgeoning trade fostered by the introduction of horses throughout the region, the ceremony spread rapidly westward and southward, reaching its fullest development during the middle of the 19th century. But the ritual was not universally accepted on the Plains. The Pawnee chose not to embrace it, a course also taken by several other village-based tribes, including the Wichita and the Omaha. Down in the Texas Panhandle, the Comanche adopted the Sun Dance in 1874, copying a simplified version from their neighbors, the Kiowa.

Despite many variations, most of the Sun Dance ceremonies sought to renew the communities' links to both spirit world and natural world. The Cheyenne even referred to the structure in which their Sun Dance was held as the New Life Lodge. According to tradition, the Cheyenne hero Erect Horns and his wife, while on a pilgrimage to the mountain where Sweet Medicine received the Sacred Arrows, were instructed to stage a sun dance in order to replenish the supply of buffalo. Similarly, in the origin story of the Gros Ventre, a hunter saw buffalo dancing in a circle and was told by the chief buffalo to adopt the dance as a "powerful means to avert sickness or danger."

The most notable exception to the theme of help and renewal was the Sun Dance performed by the Crow. In keeping with that tribe's reputation for warlike behavior, the Crow ceremony focused on revenge. The event took place only after a man vowed to sponsor it to gain vengeance for the death of a kinsman at the hands of an enemy. The mourner made

This depiction of a Teton Sioux community massed at the Sun Dance, drawn by a medicine man named Eagle Shield, includes such details as the rawhide cutouts of a man and a buffalo that customarily hung from the center pole of the dance lodge. The male figure represents a petition for victory in battle, the buffalo a prayer for plenty.

known his intention indirectly, by asking that all the buffalo tongues acquired in the hunt be saved for him. (These delicacies were traditionally fed to participants after the Sun Dance.) He then approached the owner of one of the sun dance bundles to purchase it along with the owner's services in preparing the ceremony.

The heart of the bundle was an effigy doll. Its shape having been inspired by a vision or dream, the effigy was a crude human figure encased in rawhide, stuffed with herbs and other vegetation, and frequently framed by the plume feathers from a screech owl. Because this creature symbolized impending death, it was considered a fitting helper for a mourner bent on revenge; in fact, Crow warriors often compensated the bundle owner with a horse and other goods just to allow them to wear a replica of the doll for protection in battle.

During the course of the Sun Dance, the doll would be suspended in the ceremonial lodge. With his eyes fixed upon the effigy, the mourner, who was already weakened by fasting, would dance to the point of exhaustion. Faint from effort and lack of food, he would fall into a trance and experience a powerful vision of revenge in which an enemy was killed. This signaled the conclusion of the ceremony and sometimes triggered a raid on the enemy in order to fulfill the vision.

A pledge to sponsor and perform the Sun Dance in return for some spiritual dispensation was a part of the ceremony in most Plains tribes. The Sun Dance was also the exclusive province of men. The would-be pledger of the Mandan version of the dance, known as the Okipa, not only had to be male, he also had to first dream of buffalo bulls singing Okipa songs and then win approval from a council of elders, who appraised not only his vision but his ability to come up with sufficient worldly goods to provide a suitable feast for tribal officials. Some tribes, like the Cheyenne and Gros Ventre, permitted women to pledge the event but not to actually dance; performing was left to the men.

Among the Blackfeet, however, the Sun Dance, or Medicine Lodge, could be initiated only through the vow of a woman. A woman would promise the sun to sponsor the Medicine Lodge in exchange for divine intervention in a crucial situation: a famine, for instance, or a threat of danger to family or tribe, or a sick child. If such assistance was provided, she would subsequently be called on to honor her vow and become the ceremony's Sacred Woman—but only if she met another essential qualification. Her character had to be free of any taint, especially that of adultery. Ineligible women were supposed to decline the position by saying, "No, I have a hole in my moccasin."

Honoring the promise to sponsor the Medicine Lodge turned out to be an expensive and sometimes onerous proposition. The Sacred Woman had to acquire the rights to the special *natoas* bundle, which was believed to have originated with the sun itself. The bundle contained, in addition to paints and other regalia, the ornate headdress trimmed with bird plumes and strips of white weasel skin that she would wear during the ceremony. She also was required to furnish the sacramental food, which included 100 or more tongues from buffalo bulls. The task of collecting the tongues from the hunters usually fell to the husband while she remained secluded in her tipi in meditative communion with the spirits. The Sacred Woman then presided over the ritual in which her attendants cut and prepared the tongues. Each attendant had sworn to her own marital fidelity, and the Cutting the Tongues ritual was considered a kind of test. Custom decreed a series of precise and unvarying procedures in the preparation of the delicacies; the smallest mistake would cast doubt on the veracity and virtue of the attendant.

In most Sun Dances, everyone in the village, men and women, took part at one point or another in minor roles, usually in group processions. Featured performers might range from priests and honored warriors to the pledgers and their relatives. Sioux dancers included men who were asking supernatural help for themselves or someone else, who were seeking a vision, or who wished to become a shaman. Participation in the

Many artifacts that have been used in Sun Dances are considered too sacred to show in photographs. These include the suspended effigies of man and buffalo, like those depicted in the 19th-century artwork (inset), as well as a buffalo skull and pairs of pipes, which appear on an illustrated list of the ritual's paraphernalia that was drawn up by Sioux artist Amos Bad Heart Bull.

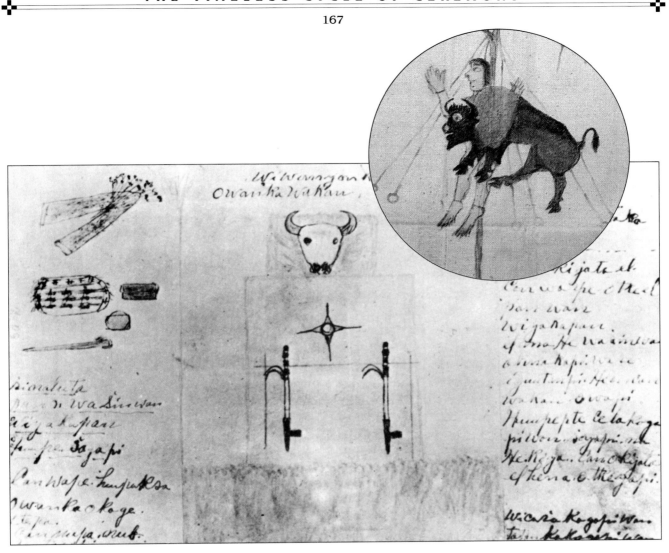

ritual was rarely as costly as in the Mandan version in which dancers in the Okipa ceremony had to either inherit the privilege or pay for it; the cooperation of the previous owners in learning the Mandan songs, chants, and rituals was imperative because the words came from an ancient dialect that was unintelligible to the tribe at large.

Each tribe signaled the beginning of the Sun Dance in its own way—none with more drama than the Mandan. Artist George Catlin, who witnessed the Okipa in 1832, wrote: "Groups of women and children were gathered on the tops of their earth-covered wigwams, and all were screaming, and dogs were howling, and all eyes directed to the prairies in the west, where was beheld at a mile distant, a solitary individual descending a prairie bluff, and making his way in a direct line toward the village! The whole community joined in the general expression of great alarm. Bows were strung and thrummed to test their elasticity. Warriors were blackening their faces and every preparation made, as if for instant combat."

When the man entered the village "with a dignified step," Catlin be-

held this "strange personage." He
was painted with white clay and
wore a headdress of raven skins
and a robe of four white wolf skins
falling back over his shoulders. He
was called Numakmaxena, or the
"Lone Man," the priest who would
preside over the beginning of the
Okipa. After greeting the chiefs and
warriors, he proceeded to the Medicine Lodge and officially opened
the door. While his assistants cleaned and prepared the structure, he
went from lodge to lodge, repeating the traditional litany: He had been
the only person saved from the calamity of the great flood, and he needed
from each household a sharp-edged tool as a sacrifice to prevent the de-
structive waters from coming again.

A depiction of a Sioux sun dance, drawn in 1910, six years after the ceremony was banned by the U.S. government, graphically illustrates two ordeals dancers endured to obtain a vision: hanging from the center pole by skewers piercing the chest and dragging buffalo skulls attached to the back.

Not all of the activities that followed the official start of the Sun
Dance would have struck the outside viewer as ceremonial in any formal
sense. The dancing itself typically required only a day or two, but the
preparations were considered an integral part of the event, and they consumed large segments of it. The Sioux did not even start construction of
the lodge where the dancing would be staged until the 10th day of their
12-day ceremony. The first four days were spent in selecting participants
and in general festivity; the next four days were devoted to instruction of
participants by the shamans in charge of the event.

The usual pattern for the nomadic tribes was to build their ceremonial lodge inside the summer camp circle, although the Blackfeet did it differently. They gathered in June for their summer encampment, but not
until August, when the chokecherries were ripe, did they officially launch
their Medicine Lodge dance. They did this by moving camp. On each of
four consecutive days, they made short marches toward the site selected
for construction of the new ceremonial lodge. More symbolic than real,
these moves were carried out as glorious dress parades in which everyone wore their finest. In the lead rode the pledger of the event, the Sacred
Woman, with the precious natoas bundle and sacramental buffalo
tongues packed on her travois and practically everything, including her
body, decorated with sacred red paint.

For other tribes as well as the Blackfeet, ceremonial precision marked
every stage of the construction process. The center pole for the lodge al-

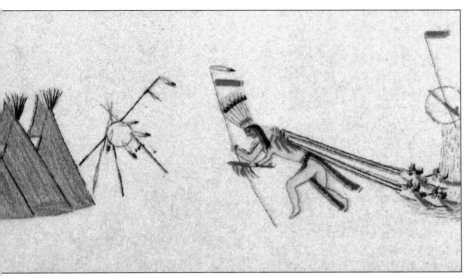

most always consisted of the trunk of a cottonwood tree with a fork near the top. The Sioux selected the cottonwood, it was said, because the pattern of its leaf provided the inspiration for the shape of the tipi. The sound that emanated from the cottonwood also inspired the Sioux; as Black Elk once expressed it, "Even in the very lightest breeze you can hear the voice of the cottonwood tree; this we understand is its prayer to the Great Spirit." The tree had to be inspected for suitability and then cut down by someone of distinction—perhaps a warrior who had recently demonstrated his courage or a maiden of unquestioned chastity.

Several tribes treated the cottonwood ceremonially as an enemy to be subdued. On the ninth day, the Sioux sent a distinguished warrior to scout the tree and mark it with red paint; on the following day, a large party of warriors rode out to "capture" the tree and bind it with rawhide thongs. After it was cut down, the trunk was likewise regarded as a fallen enemy, and young braves dashed in with war clubs and counted coup by breaking its limbs. In trimming the tree, tribesmen were careful to leave the fork at the top untouched. "The leaves must not be taken from the top," said Amos Bad Heart Bull, "for these leaves are like the scalp of mankind, and they control the spirit life of the tree."

A solemn procession bore the trunk to the construction site. The Sioux carried it on two-foot-long sticks so as to avoid touching it with their hands; approaching camp they howled like coyotes in the manner of warriors returning from the warpath. Other tribes did not allow the trunk to touch the ground until it was ceremonially dropped into the waiting hole. Sapling rafters radiated from the fork in the center pole to outer posts, which formed a circular enclosure up to 75 feet in diameter and were partially covered with brush. The Gros Ventre had a provocative custom for gathering the brush. A young man could select a woman who was not his wife to ride off with him on his horse to collect the material—assuming the husband was sufficiently confident of his wife's constancy to grant her permission to go.

The center pole would be the focus of the dancing, the hub of the symbolic little universe formed by the lodge. The Sioux and others saw the pole as a vertical link between heaven and earth. According to Arap-aho legend, it was a cosmic tree that a tribal heroine had once climbed in order to reach the upper world. In a number of the Plains tribes, buffalo skulls and other sacred objects were fastened in the fork of the center pole—sometimes even grass or willow branches to serve as a symbolic nest for some revered creature of the air. Sioux warriors, after completing the construction of the lodge on the 11th day of the ceremony, danced at the center pole, firing arrows or bullets at the rawhide effigies of a buffalo and a man hanging from the pole in order to ensure future success in hunting and war. As these dancers moved out from the pole in each of the four cardinal directions and back again, their feet smoothed the ground, stamping out the shape of a cross that would serve as a kind of altar for the climactic 12th and final day.

Other Sun Dance ceremonies moved toward a climax at their own pace and in their own particular ways. In the main ceremonial lodge and beyond it, in public and in private, the rich panoply of Plains rites revealed itself like some exotic bird of many colors. The participants sweated and smoked, chanted and danced, sang and prayed, dramatized their military exploits and rode in full-dress parades, blew upon whistles and built ritual fires, burned sweet-smelling herbs and offered up sacrifices of dried buffalo, dressed like swans or snakes and drummed incantatory rhythms that haunted the night.

The performance of the most prosaic actions—gesturing with a pipe, sketching a figure in the dirt, donning decorative paint—took on cosmic significance. In the hands of sun dance participants, the painting of face and body with a bright palette of symbolic patterns and colors became high ceremonial art—as in this tableau witnessed by George Grinnell, a noted student of the Cheyenne: "Now Bull Tongue painted the legs of Red Bead with white clay, streaking the paint by drawing his fingernails down over it. This is said to be a prayer to the snake. Afterward, his face was painted and streaked in the same way. Frank Standing Elk painted Red Bead's wife with white clay, first drawing a line of white down arms and legs, and a circle on the chest, and then smearing the paint over the whole trunk and streaking it with the fingernails. In combing the hair and in applying the paint, four motions were made before beginning. Then four streaks of white clay were drawn across the smoothed hair."

For the Cheyenne, the Sioux, and more than half of the tribes that held Sun Dances, all this built to the stunning climax. What many considered

This abandoned sun dance lodge, constructed of poplar poles, stands on the Fort Peck reservation in northeastern Montana. Still containing prayer bundles offered by dancers who made a personal sacrifice on the site, the lodge will be left to deteriorate naturally and become one with the earth again.

the true Sun Dance came typically on the final day of the event and consisted of an excruciating ordeal of self-imposed pain. The participants were volunteers, young men who underwent the so-called piercing ceremony for motives that varied by tribe and individual. A participant may have wanted to satisfy a vow made during some hazardous undertaking, show loyalty to a comrade, solicit a divine blessing, invoke a personal vision, or simply demonstrate his manhood. Whatever the motive, he was offering a sacrifice of flesh and pain. The Gros Ventre gave particular emphasis to this point by referring to the entire event as the Sacrifice Dance.

The candidates—who numbered from one or two to as many as 50—prepared by praying, fasting, and receiving instruction from priests or mentors who had previously undergone self-torture. In some tribes, they might already have danced to exhaustion in preliminary rites. Mentors then adorned them with ceremonial armor such as paint and wreaths of sage for head and wrists to ward off evil. In the Blood tribe of the Blackfoot Confederacy, a vertical row of four black dots was painted under each eye where the tears would run down.

The mentor then set about piercing the body—usually the chest, sometimes the back also. With a knife or arrowhead, he made two sets of parallel incisions on either side of the chest. In each of the resulting flaps of flesh, he inserted a wooden skewer about three inches long. On each end of the skewer he affixed a rawhide rope. Sometimes the ropes led to a buffalo skull that had to be dragged along the ground around the camp circle. More commonly, they led to the fork of the hallowed center pole in the ceremonial lodge or to a pole erected outside the lodge. Sioux and Mandan warriors sometimes volunteered to be lifted from the ground so that they actually hung in the air, suspended from the pole by rawhide rope and their own flesh. But most participants stood with feet barely touching the ground. Their agony came as they danced, jumping up and down while the blood from their wounds stained their white body paint.

Whatever the mode of torture—dragging skulls, hanging in the air, or dancing—the goal was to struggle free. The dancer threw himself around in an attempt to rip his own flesh where the wooden pegs were anchored so they would break loose. As the struggle grew desperate, spectators sang the ritual songs of pity. Photographer Edward S. Curtis wrote of the Crow ceremony he witnessed: "Some of those who had been pierced began to growl like animals and froth at the mouth and utter strange cries, while others made prophecies and described visions they were seeing."

As they suffered, Sioux dancers sought a trancelike state. They blew eagle bone whistles and gazed intently at the sun as it moved across the sky. Some achieved a state of ecstasy and revelation that carried them beyond the agony. "I blew on my eagle bone whistle in rhythm to my dancing," said Mere Left Hand Bull, a Sioux. "The sound drowned out my pain. It made me see things with my mind. I saw an eagle circling over me. At first I thought it was a dream, but then I opened my eyes and saw it was real. The eagle had heard my whistle. I became part of that eagle."

Even in this transcendent state, dancers might still remain tethered to their earthly bonds. If a dancer seemed to be suffering intolerably, or failed to break free in about an hour, an onlooker might take pity and add his own weight to increase the pressure on the ropes, or the dancer's mentor might cut the flesh further to release him. After the man was liberated, the mentor trimmed the loose skin. The dancer carried the pieces of his flesh to the base of the center pole and placed them there as a token of his suffering. The sacrifice had been made; the Sun Dance and the summer encampment were now ended. The tribe split up into smaller units for the fall hunting, their success ensured.

The self-torture of the Sun Dance stunned the handful of whites allowed to witness it during the 19th century. The Mandan version in particular was so violent—extending relentlessly over parts of several days and ending with the sacrifice of a finger—that George Catlin broke into tears as he watched. Afterward, he wrote: "Thank God, it is over, that I have seen it, and am able to tell it to the world."

Among the most conspicuous critics were the missionaries, who failed to see any parallel with the Crucifixion or traditional Christian penance. It was not just that they considered the practice of piercing barbaric; they also realized that allowing the Plains Indians to continue their own sacred practices would impede the process of converting them. During the 1880s, the United States government banned the Sun Dance on the reservations and, in 1904, deemed it and other public expressions of traditional Native American religion a punishable offense.

A few tribes continued to stage the event clandestinely, but the Sun Dance was lost to most. After the government rescinded the ban as an unnecessary restriction of freedom of religion in 1934, many Plains Indians had to consult the chronicles kept by early white ethnologists in order to relearn the long-forgotten rituals. To hold their first Sun Dance in more than 65 years, those once fearsome warriors, the Crow, received instructions from a Shoshone elder who taught them the Shoshone ceremonies.

As the old Indian ways enjoyed a resurgence of interest, even the piercing ritual was revived. The Sioux reinstituted the ordeal as part of their annual Sun Dance on the Rosebud Indian Reservation during the 1960s—just in time for the Vietnam War. In 1967 a tribesman by the name of Pete Catches vowed: "This year I want to suffer more, pierce my flesh a little deeper, dance harder, so that there may be peace, and the young men of our tribe can come home." Catches and three other volunteers then submitted to the skewers and began dancing, sacrificing their pain and some of their flesh to ask the blessing of the old Plains gods upon their brothers fighting in a faraway place.

THE CROW FAIR

For five days every August, the Crow reservation in Montana resounds with a celebration of Plains Indian culture. By the banks of the Little Bighorn River, thousands of Crows and their guests gather to camp, dance, sing, ride, renew old ties, and honor traditions that have long endured in the face of adversity.

The Crow Fair began in 1904, when the Bureau of Indian Affairs set out to re-create the sort of event staged by white farming communities, including livestock and produce shows. But Indians who met on the agency grounds for the annual fair soon transformed it into something closer in spirit to their old tribal get-togethers. Farming contests were dropped, while horse races, long favored by the Crow, took precedence—the tribal name for the fair means "racing in a circle." The event also became a showcase for traditional dancing, once banned by the government because it set Indians apart.

Over time, the fair incorporated elements of the outside culture that harmonized with Crow customs. The horse-loving fairgoers freely embraced rodeo, for example, and the Crow were the first to stage events in which all the cowboys were Indians. And modern dance steps have found their way into the festivities. But at heart, the fair remains an embodiment of ancestral values. As of old, defenders of the people occupy places of honor in ceremonies, although Crow soldiers are now joined by warriors from the political field and other public arenas. In the words of Dale Old Horn, an authority on Crow traditions, a fair that began as an exercise in assimilation has become a way for his people to "keep their culture alive and growing."

Parading by a crooked staff symbolizing courage, Crows on horseback reenact the time-honored ritual of moving camp, when the good fortune of the old site was carried to the new.

REJOINING THE TRIBAL CIRCLE

The Crow Fair echoes age-old rhythms of life on the Plains. Like other groups in the region, the Crow traditionally lived in small bands that moved often in search of game and wild growth. In summer or early fall, however, the various bands came together to hunt and conduct tribal ceremonies. The Crow Fair encampment reflects those gatherings in spirit and in structure. Pitching their tipis along the Little Bighorn River, where the Crow convened in centuries past, members of the tribe tighten their circles of kinship and community.

Youngsters frolicking along the banks of the Little Bighorn enjoy free run of the camp, just as their ancestors did in their youth.

Clustered around a stand of trees near the river, a Crow Fair encampment evokes the tribal conclaves of old.

A group of singers at the fair beats a drum fashioned of hide stretched over a circular wooden frame and decorated with the group's eagle emblem.

A Traditional Dancer performs steps that were once used by returning warriors. His proud movements mimic those of a grouse in mating season.

THE ZEST OF COMPETITION

Competition, long a driving force in the life of the Crow and other Plains peoples, figures in many events at the fair, helping to imbue traditional activities with novelty and excitement. Riders drawing on skills honed by generations of hunters and warriors contend for honors on the racetrack, cheered on by fans who have wagered on their success. And performers moving to the rhythms of drum-beating singers and wearing colorful costumes that combine traditional motifs with innovative touches vie for recognition as the finest interpreters of the various dance styles—some relatively recent and others as old as the tribe itself.

Women in richly adorned costumes dance in place, maintaining their positions in a sacred circle. In the old days, women would sway gently at the periphery like this while men danced energetically inside the circle.

Crow riders maintain the tribal tradition of racing for prizes. Plains Indians have long seen horse racing and gambling as worthy pursuits that teach men to be bold and to try their fate.

An honor guard of warriors (center) presides over the Grand Entry of all the fair's dancers, male and female, adults and children. The women at bottom, standing at the outskirts of the circle, are Traditional Dancers, while those in front of them are Fancy Shawl Dancers, whose expressive style is of more recent origin.

180

After leaping from his horse, a bull-dogging Crow cowboy digs in his heels to throw a steer. Many rodeo contestants tend livestock on land where their ancestors once pursued buffalo.

Fringes flying, a young woman takes part in a Fancy Shawl Dance. The cape worn by such dancers was adopted by the Crow from the design of a woman of the Sauk and Fox tribe.

A young man performs in the animated style called Fancy Feather dancing, devised by Oklahoma Indians in the 1950s.

INNOVATIONS FROM AFAR

The Crow Fair reflects not only local traditions but also the influence of neighboring tribes and more distant cultures. The rodeo events enjoyed at the fair originated in the cattle country of the Southwest and spread northward as cowboys took the place of buffalo hunters on the Plains. From urban dance halls came vigorous steps that left an impression on the fair's female Fancy Shawl Dancers and male Fancy Feather Dancers. Of greatest impact, however, were traditions that reached the Crow from other Indian cultures during the reservation era, when tribes overcame official barriers and looked to one another for inspiration.

Bedecked with chiming ornaments, a Jingle Dress Dancer at the fair fulfills the vision of an Ojibwa elder, who dreamed that his daughters were arrayed in medicine dresses that made marvelous sounds. When he awoke, he made the first jingles using the lids of tobacco cans.

Rounding a turn on the run, a barrel racer and her pony compete in a timed event held at the Crow Fair. Although Indian women seldom rode in pursuit of buffalo, they were good with horses, and their equestrian talents have recently been acknowledged in rodeos.

A Grass Dancer mimics the movements of windblown prairie grass— an effect accentuated by his fluttering fringes and headdress. The style was developed by a crippled Lakota, who drew strength from a vision and began to dance like grass swaying in the breeze.

A PROUD ROLL OF HONOR

The winners of contests are not the only champions at the fair. Following ancient custom, heroes are honored for defending the tribe. All the honorees are thought of as warriors, Dale Old Horn explains, but their diverse feats reflect a world where "knowledge and words have begun to take the place of military deeds and exploits." Some are elders with a lifetime of quiet service to the community. Fairgoers who have won honors then reciprocate by presenting gifts to spiritual advisers who have helped them. Personal triumphs such as the arrival of a new family member are also acknowledged with public gift giving.

Above, a racehorse wrapped in a prized Pendleton blanket awaits presentation to a prominent person being honored at the fair; many others will receive tribute in the form of blankets (top). The gift of a horse has long been regarded by Plains Indians as a mark of high esteem.

Parents introduce a toddler to the dance floor for the first time, followed by a long line of relatives. As a tribute to the honoree, friends offer welcoming gifts and then move to the end of the procession line.

Heirs to a proud warrior tradition, Crow veterans assume one of the highest honors at the fair as they present the flags to open a dance session. Service in the United States military brings the same respect once accorded those who fought for the Crow Nation in centuries past.

A CLIMACTIC PROCESSION

On the last day of the fair, the people join in a dance through the camp to consecrate their gathering. Here, as in processions of old, the Bearer of the Sacred Pipe ranks first among the leaders. After saluting Cloud Peak in the Bighorns—at the foot of which it is be- lieved holy tobacco seeds were bequeathed to the Crow by the Great Spirit—the dancers proceed to four stops representing the seasons, where their leaders offer up prayers and to- bacco smoke. Even as the dancers honor the past, they look to the future, blessing the generations to come.

Flanking the Pipe Bearer (in white hat), the four dance leaders salute Cloud Peak at the start of the procession. The sacred tobacco seeds received there long ago "possess great spiritual medicine," Dale Old Horn observes, "and bring great good fortune."

At the procession's first stop, singer Samuel Plain Feather takes up the Sacred Pipe to deliver a prayer and smoke a tobacco offering.

Holding a money tree in his left hand at the procession's third stop, dance leader Calvin Walks over the Ice moves in step to a song honoring him. In the generous spirit of the gathering, he will give the money tree to a clan father who has helped him achieve distinction.

ACKNOWLEDGMENTS

The editors wish to thank the following individuals and institutions for their valuable assistance in the preparation of this volume:

In Canada:

Alberta—Seema Bharadia, Beth Carter, The Glenbow Museum, Calgary; Ruth McConnell, Provincial Museum of Alberta, Edmonton; Chris Miller, Head-Smashed-In Buffalo Jump, Fort McLeod. British Columbia—Liz Bryan, Vancouver. Manitoba—Maureen E. Dolyniuk, Provincial Archives of Manitoba, Winnipeg.

In the United States:

Illinois: Chicago—Harvey Markowitz, D'Arcy Mc-Nickle Center, Newberry Library.

Indiana: Bloomington—Ray DeMallie, American Indian Studies Research Institute.

Maryland: Baltimore—Maria LaLima, The Walters Art Gallery.

Massachusetts: Cambridge—Martha Labell, Peabody Museum of Archaeology and Ethnology, Harvard University.

Minnesota: Saint Paul—Tracy Baker, Jean Brookins, Bonnie Wilson, Minnesota Historical Society.

Montana: Billings—Heywood Big Day. Bozeman—Bruce Selyem, Museum of the Rockies, Montana State University. Browning—Loretta Fisher-Pepion, Museum of the Plains Indian; Bob Scriver.

Nebraska: Omaha—Larry K. Mensching, Joslyn Art Museum.

New Mexico: Santa Fe—Arthur L. Olivas, Museum of New Mexico.

New York: New York—Elizabeth M. Weisberg, Art Resource.

North Dakota: Bismarck—Todd Strand, State Historical Society of North Dakota.

South Dakota: Mission—Albert White Hat, Sinte Gleska University. Rapid City—Charles Fast Horse.

Washington, D.C.: Harry Hunter, Sarah Rittgers, Division of Armed Forces History, National Museum of American History; Nicholas J. Parella, Office of Printing and Photographic Services, Smithsonian Institution.

Wyoming: Cody—Emma Hansen, Elizabeth Holmes, Tina Stopka, Buffalo Bill Historical Center. Laramie—Charles A. Reher, Department of Anthropology, University of Wyoming.

BIBLIOGRAPHY

BOOKS

Albers, Patricia, and Beatrice Medicine, *The Hidden Half: Studies of Plains Indian Women.* Lanham, Md.: University Press of America, 1983.

Andrews, Elaine, *Indians of the Plains.* New York: Facts On File, 1992.

Bamforth, Douglas B., *Ecology and Human Organization on the Great Plains.* New York: Plenum Press, 1988.

Bancroft-Hunt, Norman, *The Indians of the Great Plains.* London: Orbis Publishing, 1985.

Barsness, Larry, *The Bison in Art: A Graphic Chronicle of the American Bison.* Flagstaff, Ariz.: Northland Press, 1977.

Bebbington, Julia M., *Quillwork of the Plains.* Calgary: Glenbow-Alberta Institute, 1982.

Beck, Peggy V., Anna Lee Walters, and Nia Francisco, *The Sacred: Ways of Knowledge, Sources of Life.* Tsaile, Ariz.: Navajo Community College Press, 1992.

Billard, Jules B., ed., *The World of the American Indian.* Washington, D.C.: National Geographic Society, 1989.

Bodmer, Karl, *Karl Bodmer's America.* Omaha: University of Nebraska Press, 1984.

Bowers, Alfred W., *Mandan Social and Ceremonial Organization.* Chicago: University of Chicago Press, 1950.

Brown, Joseph Epes, ed., *The Sacred Pipe: Black Elk's Account of the Seven Rites of the Oglala Sioux.* Norman: University of Oklahoma Press, 1953.

Bryan, Liz, *The Buffalo People: Prehistoric Archaeology on the Canadian Plains.* Edmonton: University of Alberta Press, 1991.

Capps, Benjamin, and the Editors of Time-Life Books, *The Indians.* (The Old West series). Alexandria, Va.: Time-Life Books, 1973.

Catlin, George, *Letters and Notes on the Manners, Customs, and Conditions of the North American Indians.* Vols. 1 and 2. New York: Dover Publications, 1973.

Charging Eagle, Tom, and Ron Zeilinger, *Black Hills: Sacred Hills.* Chamberlain, S.Dak.: Tipi Press, 1987.

Collins, Richard, ed., *The Native Americans: The Indigenous People of North America.* New York: Smithmark Publishers, 1991.

Conn, Richard, *Circles of the World: Traditional Art of the Plains Indians.* Denver: Denver Art Museum, 1982.

Cooper, John M., *The Gros Ventres of Montana. Part II: Religion and Ritual.* Ed. by Regina Flannery. Washington, D.C.: Catholic University of America Press, 1957.

DeMallie, Raymond J., and Douglas R. Parks, eds., *Sioux Indian Religion: Tradition and Innovation.* Norman: University of Oklahoma Press, 1987.

The Editors of Time-Life Books, *The Spirit World.* (The American Indians series). Alexandria, Va.: Time-Life Books, 1992.

Erdoes, Richard:

Crying for a Dream: The World through Native American Eyes. Santa Fe, N.Mex.: Bear & Company, 1990.

The Sun Dance People: The Plains Indians, Their Past and Present. New York: Random House, 1972.

Ewers, John C.:

Blackfeet Indians: Ethnological Report on the Blackfeet and Gros Ventre Tribes of Indians. New York: Garland Publishing, 1974.

The Horse in Blackfoot Indian Culture. Washington, D.C.: Smithsonian Institution Press, 1955.

Indian Life on the Upper Missouri. Norman: University of Oklahoma Press, 1968.

Freedman, Russell, *Buffalo Hunt.* New York: Holiday House, 1988.

Frey, Rodney, *The World of the Crow Indians: As Driftwood Lodges.* Norman: University of Oklahoma Press, 1987.

Gill, Sam D., *Native American Traditions: Sources*

and Interpretations. Belmont, Calif.: Wadsworth Publishing, 1983.

Gilman, Carolyn, and Mary Jane Schneider, *The Way to Independence: Memories of a Hidatsa Indian Family, 1840-1920.* St. Paul: Minnesota Historical Society Press, 1987.

Green Rayna, *Women in American Indian Society.* Ed. by Frank W. Porter III. New York: Chelsea House Publishers, 1992.

Grinnell, George Bird, *The Cheyenne Indians: Their History and Ways of Life.* Vols. 1 and 2. Lincoln: University of Nebraska Press, 1972 (reprint of 1923 edition).

Gussow, Zachary, *Cheyenne and Arapaho Aboriginal Occupation.* New York: Garland Publishing, 1974.

Haines, Francis:
The Buffalo. New York: Thomas Y. Crowell, 1970.
The Plains Indians. New York: Thomas Y. Crowell, 1976.

Harrod, Howard L., *Renewing the World: Plains Indian Religion and Morality.* Tucson: University of Arizona Press, 1987.

Hassrick, Royal B., *The Sioux: Life and Customs of a Warrior Society.* Norman: University of Oklahoma Press, 1964.

Hirschfelder, Arlene, and Paulette Molin, *The Encyclopedia of Native American Religions: An Introduction.* New York: Facts On File, 1992.

Hoig, Stan, *The Cheyenne.* Ed. by Frank W. Porter III. New York: Chelsea House Publishers, 1989.

Holder, Preston, *The Hoe and the Horse on the Plains: A Study of Cultural Development among North American Indians.* Lincoln: University of Nebraska Press, 1970.

Hoover, Herbert T., *The Yankton Sioux.* Ed. by Frank W. Porter III. New York: Chelsea House Publishers, 1988.

Hoxie, Frederick E., *The Crow.* Ed. by Frank W. Porter III. New York: Chelsea House Publishers, 1989.

Hultkrantz, Åke, *Native Religions of North America: The Power of Visions and Fertility.* San Francisco: Harper, 1987.

Iverson, Peter, ed., *The Plains Indians of the Twentieth Century.* Norman: University of Oklahoma Press, 1985.

Jenness, Diamond, *The Indians of Canada.* Toronto: University of Toronto Press, 1977.

Jennings, Jesse D., ed., *Ancient Native Americans.* San Francisco: W. H. Freeman, 1978.

Josephy, Alvin M., Jr., ed., *The American Heritage Book of Indians.* New York: Bonanza Books, 1988.

Kinietz, W. Vernon, *The Indians of the Western Great Lakes: 1615-1760.* Ann Arbor: University of Michigan Press, 1965.

Kroeber, Alfred Louis, *Ethnology of the Gros Ventre.* New York: AMS Press, 1978 (reprint of 1908 edition).

Lame Deer, Archie Fire, and Richard Erdoes, *Gift of Power: The Life and Teachings of a Lakota Medicine Man.* Santa Fe, N.Mex.: Bear & Company, 1992.

LaPointe, James, *Legends of the Lakota.* San Francisco: Indian Historian Press, 1976.

Laubin, Reginald, and Gladys Laubin:
Indian Dances of North America: Their Importance to Indian Life. Norman: University of Oklahoma Press, 1977.
The Indian Tipi: Its History, Construction, and Use. Norman: University of Oklahoma Press, 1977.

Lowie, Robert H.:
The Crow Indians. Lincoln: University of Nebraska Press, 1983.
Indians of the Plains. Lincoln: University of Nebraska Press, 1982.

McCracken, Harold, *George Catlin and the Old Frontier.* New York: Bonanza Books, 1959.

Murie, James R., *Ceremonies of the Pawnee.* Ed. by Douglas R. Parks. Lincoln: University of Nebraska Press, 1981.

Nabokov, Peter, and Robert Easton, *Native American Architecture.* New York: Oxford University Press, 1989.

Paper, Jordan, *Offering Smoke: The Sacred Pipe and Native American Religion.* Edmonton: University of Alberta Press, 1989.

Penney, David W., ed., *Art of the American Indian Frontier: The Chandler-Pohrt Collection.* Seattle: University of Washington Press, 1992.

Phillips, Paul Chrisler, *The Fur Trade.* Vol. 2. Norman: University of Oklahoma Press, 1961.

Plummer, Norman B., *The Crow Tribe of Indians.* New York: Garland Publishing, 1974.

Pond, Samuel W., *The Dakota or Sioux in Minnesota As They Were in 1834.* St. Paul: Minnesota Historical Society Press, 1986.

Powell, Peter J., *Sweet Medicine: The Continuing Role of the Sacred Arrows, the Sun Dance, and the Sacred Buffalo Hat in Northern Cheyenne History.* Vols. 1 and 2. Norman: University of Oklahoma Press, 1969.

Powers, William K., *Oglala Religion.* Lincoln: University of Nebraska Press, 1977.

Rezatto, Helen, *Tales of the Black Hills.* Rapid City, S.Dak.: Fenwyn Press, 1989.

Roe, Frank Gilbert, *The Indian and the Horse.* Norman: University of Oklahoma Press, 1955.

Schneider, Mary Jane, *The Hidatsa.* Ed. by Frank W. Porter III. New York: Chelsea House Publishers, 1989.

Schuon, Frithjof, *The Feathered Sun: Plains Indians in Art and Philosophy.* Bloomington, Ind.: World Wisdom Books, 1990.

Scriver, Bob, *The Blackfeet: Artists of the Northern Plains: The Scriver Collection of Blackfeet Indian Artifacts and Related Objects, 1894-1990.* Kansas City, Mo.: Lowell Press, 1990.

Tillett, Leslie, ed., *Wind on the Buffalo Grass: The Indians' Own Account of the Battle at the Little Big Horn River, & the Death of Their Life on the Plains.* New York: Thomas Y. Crowell, 1976.

Underhill, Ruth Murray, *Red Man's America: A History of Indians in the United States.* Chicago: University of Chicago Press, 1971.

Voget, Fred W., *The Shoshoni-Crow Sun Dance.* Norman: University of Oklahoma Press, 1984.

Walker, James R., *Lakota Belief and Ritual.* Ed. by Raymond J. DeMallie and Elaine A. Jahner. Lincoln: University of Nebraska Press, 1991.

Walton, Ann T., John C. Ewers, and Royal B. Hassrick, *After the Buffalo Were Gone: The Louis Warren Hill, Sr., Collection of Indian Art.* St. Paul, Minn.: Northwest Area Foundation, 1985.

Webb, Walter Prescott, *The Great Plains.* Lincoln: University of Nebraska Press, 1959.

Wedel, Waldo R., *Prehistoric Man on the Great Plains.* Norman: University of Oklahoma Press, 1961.

Wilson, Gilbert L., *The Horse and the Dog in Hidatsa Culture.* Vol. 15, part 2 of *Anthropological Papers of the American Museum of Natural History.* New York: American Museum Press, 1980 (reprint of 1924 edition).

Wood, W. Raymond, and Thomas D. Thiessen, eds., *Early Fur Trade on the Northern Plains: Canadian Traders among the Mandan and Hidatsa Indians, 1738-1818.* Norman: University of Oklahoma Press, 1985.

Woolworth, Alan R., and John L. Champe, *Ethnohistorical Report on the Yankton Sioux: Sioux Indians 3.* New York: Garland Publishing, 1974.

Yellowtail, Thomas, *Yellowtail, Crow Medicine Man and Sun Dance Chief: An Autobiography As Told to Michael Oren Fitzgerald.* Norman: University of Oklahoma Press, 1991.

Yue, David, and Charlotte Yue, *The Tipi: A Center of Native American Life.* New York: Alfred A. Knopf, 1984.

PERIODICALS

Bunge, Robert P., "The American Indian: A Natural Philosopher." *Intellect,* June 1978.

Frison, George C., "The Buffalo Pound in Northwestern Plains Prehistory: Site 48 CA 302, Wyoming." *American Antiquity,* January 1971.

Haase, Eric, "Tatanka: A Quest for Cultural Survival." *Lakota Times,* April 8, 1992.

Reeves, B. O. K., "Six Millenniums of Buffalo Kills." *Scientific American,* October 1983.

Wilson, Gilbert Livingstone, "Agriculture of the Hidatsa Indians: An Indian Interpretation." *Bulletin of the University of Minnesota,* November 1917.

OTHER PUBLICATIONS

"1992 Annual Crow Fair." Newspaper. November 1992.

Black Boy, Cecile, "Blackfeet Tipi Legends," in *Painted Tipis by Contemporary Plains Indian Artists.* Museum Exhibition Catalog. Anadarko: Oklahoma Indian Arts and Crafts Cooperative, 1973.

Densmore, Frances, "Teton Sioux Music." *Smithsonian Institution, Bureau of American Ethnology, Bulletin 61.* Washington, D.C.: Government Printing Office, 1918.

Hau, Kóla!: The Plains Indian Collection of the Haffenreffer Museum of Anthropology. Museum Exhibition Catalog. Bristol, R.I.: Haffenreffer Museum of Anthropology, Brown University, 1983.

McClintock, Walter, "Blackfoot Warrior Societies." Monograph. *Southwest Museum Leaflets.* Los Angeles: Southwest Museum, 1937.

Maurer, Evan M., ed., *Visions of the People: A Pictorial History of Plains Indian Life.* Museum Exhibition Catalog. Minneapolis, Minn.: The Minneapolis Institute of Arts, 1992.

Reher, Charles A., "Basic Information Packet for Discussion of a Site Development Plan." Laramie: University of Wyoming Vore Buffalo Jump Research Center, 1992.

Sacred Circles: Two Thousand Years of North American Indian Art. Museum Exhibition Catalog. Kansas City, Mo.: Nelson Gallery of Art-Atkins Museum of Fine Arts, 1977.

PICTURE CREDITS

The sources for the illustrations that appear in this book are listed below. Credits from left to right are separated by semicolons; from top to bottom they are separated by dashes.

Cover: Joslyn Art Museum, Omaha, Nebraska. **6, 7:** Courtesy Prairie Edge, Rapid City, South Dakota—© Jerry Jacka. **8:** Courtesy Maxwell Museum of Anthropology. **9:** State Historical Society of North Dakota; Library of Congress, USZ62-96195. **10:** Library of Congress; National Anthropological Archives (NAA), Smithsonian Institution, Washington, D.C., neg. no. 4650. **11:** Haynes Foundation Collection, Montana Historical Society, photographed by F. Jay Haynes; Library of Congress. **12:** Photo by Joseph A. Dixon, courtesy Museum of New Mexico, neg. no. 68011; photo by DeLancey Gill, courtesy Museum of New Mexico, neg. no. 59439. **13:** NAA, Smithsonian Institution, Washington, D.C., neg. no. 303B; Western History Collections, University of Oklahoma Library. **15:** National Museum of American Art, Smithsonian Institution, Washington, D.C./Art Resource, New York. **16:** Map by Maryland CartoGraphics, Inc. **17:** State Historical Society of North Dakota. **20:** Minnesota Historical Society. **22:** Buffalo Bill Historical Center, Cody, Wyoming/gift of Mr. and Mrs. Irving H. "Larry" Larom—NAA, Smithsonian Institution, Washington, D.C., neg. no. 75-10315. **23:** Buffalo Bill Historical Center, Cody, Wyoming/gift of Mr. and Mrs. Irving H. "Larry" Larom. **24:** Map by Maryland CartoGraphics, Inc. **26:** Peabody Museum, Harvard University, photo by Hillel Burger, photo no. T941c. **27:** Denver Art Museum, acquisition no. 1985.45. **28, 29:** Buffalo Bill Historical Center, Wyoming/Chandler-Pohrt Collection. **30:** From *The Hidatsa Earthlodge*, Anthropological Papers of the American Museum of Natural History, 1934; Minnesota Historical Society. **31:** Minnesota Historical Society—Minnesota Historical Society, Museum Collections, photographed by Peter Latner—neg. no. 286579, courtesy Department of Library Services, American Museum of Natural History—Minnesota Historical Society, Museum Collections, photographed by Peter Latner. **32:** Minnesota Historical Society—neg. no. 286444, courtesy Department of Library Services, American Museum of Natural History. **33:** Minnesota Historical Society; Minnesota Historical Society, Museum Collections, photographed by Peter Latner—Minnesota Historical Society—from *Agriculture of the Hidatsa Indians: an Indian Interpretation* by Gilbert L. Wilson, University of Minnesota, Minneapolis, 1917. **36, 37:** Larry Sherer, courtesy National Museum of American History, Smithsonian Institution, Washington, D.C.—courtesy Panhandle Plains Historical Society, Canyon, Texas; from *The Blackfeet: Artists of the Northern Plains* by Bob Scriver, Lowell Press, Kansas City, Missouri, 1990; Buffalo Bill Historical Center, Cody, Wyoming. **39:** © The Detroit Institute of Arts, gift of Mr. and Mrs. Pohrt. **43:** © Tom Till. **44, 45:** © Dick Dietrich Photography. **46-49:** © Eric Haase. **50, 51:** © Michael Crummett. **52, 53:** © Eric Haase. **54:** NAA, Smithsonian Institution,

Washington, D.C., neg. no. 75-11743. **56, 57:** Joslyn Art Museum, Omaha, Nebraska. **58:** Buffalo Bill Historical Center, Cody, Wyoming/gift of Mr. and Mrs. Irving H. "Larry" Larom. **60, 61:** Trans. no. 4632(2), photo by Dennis Finnin, courtesy Department of Library Services, American Museum of Natural History; Larry Sherer. **62:** © Michael Crummett. **64, 65:** Richard Erdoes—Larry Sherer. **66:** Richard and Marion Pohrt (92). **68:** NAA, Smithsonian Institution, Washington, D.C., neg. no. 76-4346. **69:** Buffalo Bill Historical Center, Cody, Wyoming/gift of Mr. and Mrs. Irving H. "Larry" Larom. **70, 71:** Buffalo Bill Historical Center, Cody, Wyoming/gift of Nick Eggenhofer—Denver Art Museum, acquisition no. 1938.322. **73:** Courtesy of Glenbow, Calgary, Alberta. **76:** John Anderson Collection, South Dakota State Historical Society, State Archives, Pierre; Larry Sherer. **77:** Collection of Glenbow, Calgary, Alberta, AF2358B—AF 2389—Steve Fischbach; Herbert T. Hoover. **78:** Richard Erdoes—courtesy Haffenreffer Museum of Anthropology, Brown University, Bristol, Rhode Island. **79:** Collection of Glenbow, Calgary, Alberta, AF289 A-B—AF2321A-B. **80:** Courtesy of Glenbow, Calgary, Alberta. **81:** Trans. no. 4270, photo by Craig Chesek, courtesy Department of Library Services, American Museum of Natural History. **82:** Buffalo Bill Historical Center, Cody, Wyoming. **83:** NAA, Smithsonian Institution, Washington, D.C., neg. no. 76-15155. **84:** © Museum of the Rockies/Bruce Selyem. **85-93:** © Michael Crummett. **94, 95:** Field Museum of Natural History, Chicago, neg. no. A111349c—Richard Erdoes. **96:** Trans. no. 4719(2), photo by Dennis Finnin, courtesy Department of Library Services, American Museum of Natural History. **97:** Joslyn Art Museum, Omaha, Nebraska. **100:** Minnesota Historical Society. **101:** Buffalo Bill Historical Center, Cody, Wyoming/gift of Mr. and Mrs. Irving H. "Larry" Larom. **102:** NAA, Smithsonian Institution, Washington, D.C., neg. no. 55-940. **103:** Courtesy Haffenreffer Museum of Anthropology, Brown University, Bristol, Rhode Island. **104:** Liz Bryan. **105:** The Walters Art Gallery, Baltimore, Maryland. **106:** Item no. H89.220.489.2a-c, courtesy Ethnology Program, Provincial Museum of Alberta, Edmonton—item no. H88.94.172, courtesy Ethnology Program, Provincial Museum of Alberta, Edmonton. **107:** Courtesy Dr. Charles A. Reher, University of Wyoming. **108:** NAA, Smithsonian Institution, Washington, D.C., neg. no. 3701—Richard Erdoes. **110:** Item no. H89.220.89.2c, courtesy Ethnology Program, Provincial Museum of Alberta, Edmonton; The Science Museum of Minnesota, Saint Paul—item no. H89.220.377.8b-e, courtesy Ethnology Program, Provincial Museum of Alberta, Edmonton. **111:** Item no. H65.14.7q, courtesy Ethnology Program, Provincial Museum of Alberta, Edmonton. **112:** Item no. H89.220.72, courtesy Ethnology Program, Provincial Museum of Alberta, Edmonton—item no. H67.251.19, courtesy Ethnology Program, Provincial Museum of Alberta, Edmonton. **113:** Minnesota Historical Society, Museum Collections, photographed by Peter Latner. **114, 115:** Trans. no. 3273(2), photo by Lee Boltin, courtesy Department of Library Services, American Museum of Natural History—National Museum of American Art,

Smithsonian Institution, Washington, D.C./Art Resource, New York. **118, 119:** Art by Karen Barnes of Wood, Ronsaville, Harlin Inc. **121:** Courtesy DeGolyer Library, Southern Methodist University, Dallas—courtesy of Glenbow, Calgary, Alberta—Jerry Jacka, courtesy Ginger K. Renner, Paradise Valley, Arizona. **122, 123:** © Eric Haase. **124, 125:** Southwest Museum, Los Angeles, MCC.402. **126, 127:** Buffalo Bill Historical Center, Cody, Wyoming/Richard A. Pohrt Collection (5)—Museum für Volkerkunde, Staatliche Museen Preussischer Kulturbesitz, Berlin, photo Dietrich Graf. **128:** The Science Museum of Minnesota, Saint Paul. **129:** Buffalo Bill Historical Center, Cody, Wyoming/gift of Anne Black; Little Bighorn Battlefield National Monument—art by Rob Wood of Wood, Ronsaville, Harlin Inc. **130, 131:** Art by Rob Wood of Wood, Ronsaville, Harlin Inc.; Buffalo Bill Historical Center, Cody, Wyoming (2)—from *The Blackfeet: Artists of the Northern Plains* by Bob Scriver, Lowell Press, Kansas City, Missouri, 1990. **132:** Courtesy of Glenbow, Calgary, Alberta; courtesy Haffenreffer Museum of Anthropology, Brown University, Bristol, Rhode Island. **133:** Denver Art Museum, acquisition no. 1940.136; State Historical Society of North Dakota—Denver Art Museum, acquisition no. 1956.162. **134:** Item no. H65.84.1a-c, 2a, courtesy Ethnology Program, Provincial Museum of Alberta, Edmonton. **135-139:** U.S. Department of Interior, Indian Arts and Crafts Board, Museum of the Plains Indian, photographed by Joe Fisher. **140, 141:** State Historical Society of North Dakota—© Tom Till. **142:** Collection of Glenbow, Calgary, Alberta, AF83. **144, 145:** © Michael Crummett. **148, 149:** NAA, Smithsonian Institution, Washington, D.C., neg. no. 34054-0. **150, 151:** NAA, Smithsonian Institution, Washington, D.C., neg. no. 3434-E-4. **152, 153:** © Tom Till; Buffalo Bill Historical Center, Cody, Wyoming/Adolf Spohr Collection, gift of Mr. Larry Sheerin—Peabody Museum, Harvard University, photo by Hillel Burger, photo no. T1267a. **154, 155:** Dennis L. Sanders/Hardin Photo Service, Hardin, Montana. **157:** From *Wind on the Buffalo Grass* edited by Leslie Tillett, Thomas Y. Crowell, New York, 1976. **158, 159:** National Museum of American Art, Smithsonian Institution, Washington, D.C./Art Resource, New York; courtesy Haffenreffer Museum of Anthropology, Brown University, Bristol, Rhode Island. **160, 161:** From *The Blackfeet: Artists of the Northern Plains* by Bob Scriver, Lowell Press, Kansas City, Missouri, 1990. **163:** Richard Erdoes. **165:** From *Teton Sioux Music* by Frances Densmore, Smithsonian Institution, Washington, D.C., 1918. **167:** From *Wind on the Buffalo Grass* edited by Leslie Tillett, Thomas Y. Crowell, New York, 1976, inset Richard Erdoes. **168, 169:** From *Teton Sioux Music* by Frances Densmore, Smithsonian Institution, Washington, D.C., 1918. **170, 171:** © Michael Crummett. **174, 175:** © Michael Crummett. **176, 177:** © Tom Kochel. **178, 179:** © Tom Kochel (2); © Michael Crummett (3). **180:** © Michael Crummett—© Tom Kochel (2). **181, 182:** © Michael Crummett. **183:** © Michael Crummett—© Tom Kochel. **184, 185:** © Michael Crummett.

INDEX

Numerals in italics indicate an illustration of the subject mentioned.